Also By Alex Stokes

Messing With Tourists
Stupid Answers To Stupid Questions

Best Wishes,
and Enjoy!

Alex Glenn
2016

5 Years Of This?

Husband. Father. Comedian.
My Story.

Alex Stokes

ISBN-13: 978-1508553243
ISBN-10: 1508553246

Dedication

Once again, I would like to dedicate this book first and foremost to my wonderful wife Jenny. Without her full support I wouldn't be able to pursue this crazy dream. Also, to my incredible family, who have always been there for me throughout all the stupid and completely irrational life decisions I seem to make every so often. When I said family, I also meant my children, the cat, and the puppy. Last, but not least, all my amazing friends who support me by coming to shows, buying my books, and liking my online stupidity. Oh, and to that one guy who says he's an actual fan, thank you.

Contents

Introduction

Also, I don't have an editor. I do it myself. Yes, I was an English Major. However, who cares. I write like it's a conversation. Sometimes it's just short and sweet sentences. Period. Just like the last one I just typed. Remember, I'm a comedian, not an author.

There are many, many great books out there by famous comedians and entertainers, both about their lives and the business itself. They tell of crazy stories (many sad and depressing) of how they had to struggle to just make it. I've always found stories like those fascinating and also great learning experiences.

Everyone has a cool story, an interesting history, a background full of fascinating tales that led them to be the person they are today. Artists of all nature, in particular, seem to have followed paths that most would cringe at, yet they want to hear more about. There are also many who think that stand-up comedians are the weirdest of them all. I'm not here to say they are. I'm not going to dispute it, either.

So, why would a guy who is a "not so well known" comedian write a book about his life and career and think people would actually want to read it? I don't have the answer. Maybe you guys can tell me after you read it.

My story is of a husband, a father, a genuine "good guy", who is trying to make it as a stand-up Comedian while at the same time being a husband, father, and "good guy." I don't live in L.A. I don't live in New York. I don't live in Chicago. No, I live in Knoxville, TN. The first 5 years alone trying to make it in this crazy business have filled notebook after notebook full of interesting stories, both good and bad. On one hand, I've been lucky and have had some great things fall my way so early in my career. On the other hand, just weirdness. Nothing really bad, just weird.

So, what is my goal in telling this story? To inspire others to do what I've done? Maybe. Is it to encourage people to *not* do what I've done? Maybe. Is it just to write another book because I'm bored? Maybe. In all honesty, my main goal is to show everyone that there are different paths that people take to make it in every profession, for many different reasons. The world of stand-up comedy is no different. There are the touring "Comedy Club" comics, the touring "Underground" comics, public speakers and corporate entertainers. There are crossbreeds and overachievers and underachievers of all the above. To be honest, I couldn't really tell you where I fall. I am, and always have been, taking my own path to make it. This isn't necessarily by choice, as you will read later, but it's the way it is.

The perspective of my story is going to be a little different from other books out there by famous comedians and artists. My story is ongoing. I'm just beginning. It's been a wild ride so far, but there is a long way to go. I hope you join me after reading this. Come to a show, say hi. Tell me your stories. Hopefully, in about 5 years, you will be reading another book called "10 Years Of This?" by a guy that doesn't have to write an introduction explaining who he is and why he wrote it.

So, take a seat. Get comfortable. Grab some wine or a beer or both. Prepare to laugh, cry, and possibly throw this book across the room. Just remember this....

I'm not a writer. I'm a comedian. I don't have an editor. This is just me. This is real. I don't need someone else to change my story. I'm writing this as I feel it needs to be written. Enjoy.

How Did I Get Here?

I'm not stupid. I know most of you don't care about the non-comedy part of my life. However, the comedy part doesn't exist without the rest of it. So, you are just going to have to bear through this, read it, and like it. Or, just skip ahead.

The Roller Skating Years

Since the age of 3, I have lived in East Tennessee. My first aspirations were to be a professional roller skater. Until the age of 10, my family either owned or operated skating rinks in both Florida and Oak Ridge, TN. This was my life. Every day. All day long. Roller Skating.

Oh, and I was really, really good at it too. I competed in regional speed skating competitions, could do tricks like no one else my age, and loved every second of it. I lived at that skating rink. When I wasn't skating, I was playing unlimited amounts of video games like Asteroids and Donkey Kong (way better than what kids have today...I had an entire arcade at my disposal and my dad was the boss. So there.) I competed in Air Band competitions on the weekends to the likes of Loverboy and the J. Geils Band. Yeah, my early childhood was pretty sweet.

I was born at Eglen Air Force Base in Florida. Both my mother and father were in the Air Force, which is probably why I was born there. I'm figuring all this out with you guys as we go along. My grandparents had a skating rink nearby in Milton, FL. My mother was a record breaking speed skater as a child, so naturally I was destined to carry on this strange tradition.

Competing in a regional speed skating competition. I'm pretty sure that's me in second place. It's hard to tell. We were all wearing knee high socks and helmets. In that case, just pretend I'm in first.

A few years after we had moved to Tennessee, I started going back to Milton to train at my grandparents' skating rink. It was a small, hot skating rink, and it was surrounded by Willow Trees and snakes. My grandfather trained me and several other children during the summer. Here is what I remember about those "training" sessions. I went around in a thousand circles during the day, got yelled at a lot (My grandfather was a tough competitor), and then I went back to my grandparents' house to eat Perogies. Tons of Russian blood on that side of my family. As hard as it was, I still enjoyed every second of it, and I'm pretty sure that that competitive environment has stuck with me to this day.

The Basketball Era

Somewhere around 1983, at the age of 10, we moved from Oak Ridge to Sevierville, TN. This would be the end of my roller skating career.

Originally, we moved there for my dad to take over another skating rink in Pigeon Forge. For reasons that I can't remember, it was short lived. Luckily, in second grade back in Oak Ridge, I had also fallen in love with the game of basketball. This...this would be my new life.

My first day of tryouts at Sevierville Middle School for the 5th and 6th grade basketball team, I showed up wearing artificial turf cleats. Once again, my memory is not exactly clear as to *why* I was wearing them. I do remember, however, that I felt like a cool outsider. The rest of the kids were both baffled and intrigued. It was like I came from another world that played a very different sport.

The next 7 of years of my life, up until the end of my junior year of High School, I played basketball 24/7. I did the same my senior year as well, but I'm saving that for another paragraph (it's the good part.) Let's focus on the 7 years first. I spent this period playing basketball all the time, by myself, pick-up games at the park, camps, practice, in my bedroom with the trash can. Anywhere, everywhere, all the time. I was developing skills that nobody else around me had. Unfortunately, my confidence wasn't catching up.

During this time, I was learning more about myself than I realized. I was playing on very successful basketball teams, but as a back-up. I was confused, because I knew how good I was. I just couldn't figure out why I wasn't "the man." It was at times very difficult, however, those struggles have stuck with me to this day. I have an appreciation for working hard, being the best, but being patient. (See...I told you guys that there was relevance from my non-comedy life.)

Sure, I'm a pretty laid back guy. Always have been. I can get complacent and just enjoy being in the middle of all the hoopla (I'm not sure if I intended that pun or not.) I know I was guilty of that during those 7 years, just as I have been guilty during every other stage of my life, including comedy. I always seem to find a way, however, of pulling through in the end.

So, fast forward to my senior year of High School. I guess you could say I was popular, although in my eyes I was just a goofy, skinny kid who got along with everyone. Also, by the time my senior year rolled around, I had fully eliminated my mullet. Sure, I'll put a pic of it in here for you.

I'm really not sure that this was a good idea. Oh well, too late. Mullet, circa 1990.

Now, I could easily spend 14 chapters on my senior year of High School, especially the basketball part. Instead, let me just give you the highlight reel. The season began, and it was finally my time to be a starter! I had waited for this since 5th grade. It was partially due to my skills, and also the fact that a ton of guys graduated and I was what was left. Either way, I decided to make the most of it. It was an up and down season. I was great for a few games, then I would disappear.

Late in the season, something happened that would change everything. During a game, I passed out, and it was determined that I had a previously unknown heart condition. Nothing too serious, as it would turn out, but I would miss several games out of precaution. If it was up to my mother, I would have been done, period.

During this time, I reflected and thought about how much I missed playing. I would sit on the bench and watch. It was difficult, but it also gave me a greater appreciation for not being able to do what I loved. By the way folks, this is another analogy that's going to pop up later in the book.

By the time the tournaments rolled around, I was ready, and I was better than I had ever been. I was aggressive and finally just showed what I could do. I had a string of some of the best games of my life.

Then, in one magical moment, I found myself standing on the court in the biggest game in school history. It was the Sub State...one game away from going to the State Tournament. No school in Sevier County history had ever been to the State Tournament at that time, and nobody thought we would be going either.

With seconds left, and the game tied at 50, I was fortunate enough to be in the right place at the right time. I stole the ball from the guy I was guarding, knocked it to a teammate, sprinted down the court, he threw it back to me, and I hit the game winning shot to send us to State. It was a magical moment, a magical night. The kind of night I can't wait to have again in comedy. I know it's coming. I just have to keep pushing and stay patient.

Confusing the defender with my Pigeon Toed jump shot. Distracted him just long enough.

The Many, Many College Years

After a wonderful run through High School, it was time to move on to real life. Apparently, the guy that this book is about wasn't quite ready for that.

There were a few scholarships coming my way for basketball, mostly small colleges and a couple small Division 1 schools. However, at this point I was tired of basketball. 11 years of practice, wear and tear on my body, and just having no "extra" time to be myself was taking its toll. I wasn't really sure what I wanted to do. I just knew that I wasn't ready to play basketball, at least for a while.

So, I did what I was best at. I procrastinated. Until the very last minute. I ended up going to a small Junior College nearby with my 2 best friends. 18 years old, not sure what I was doing. I just knew I wanted to hang out with them. That was pretty much it. No aspirations at this point. Forget basketball. Just hang out and have some fun.

It was roughly an hour drive to school every day. We would hop in my Plymouth Laser, listen to the Judybats (our favorite band that just happened to be from Knoxville) on the way there, skip half of our classes, listen to the Judybats on the way back, and that was it. We played intramural basketball to keep ourselves somewhat active. The rest of the time it was Mountain Dew and Tecmo Bowl on the Nintendo. It was actually quite invigorating for 1992.

Surprisingly, my grades were really good that first year. I don't really know how that happened, seeing that I rarely actually attended class. Also, during this first year, I took a Speech class. Being that I am now a stand-up comedian, it's funny to think about how petrified I was speaking in front of 20 other students. Matter of fact, I think that was my worst grade. While goofy and fun around my friends, I was not exactly a public speaker at age 18. My semi-breakout moment came while giving a speech about my boxer shorts, and displaying them to the rest of the class. I guess we shall call this the beginning?

Sometime during that first year, the head coach at this Junior College noticed me playing intramural basketball. He convinced me to join the team the next year on scholarship. To be honest, I was kind of missing the structure of playing basketball full time. Let me emphasize the words "kind of." I really wasn't sure of what I was doing at that time. I was a very impressionable young man, who had no aspirations. I was just living life, enjoying time with my friends. I remember thinking, hey... let's give this a try...you practiced all your life to play college basketball, right?

So, year 2 rolls around. It's time for me to move to my new apartment. Unlike kids today, I was not prepared for this. I borrowed my best friend's truck, which was tiny, and packed up my furniture. I knew I was going to have 3 roommates from the team. The only one I knew was my good friend Mark Newman from my high school team.

About a mile from my parent's house, I take a turn in this truck, with all my furniture in the back, and it falls out. Now, since I was apparently a moron, I didn't even notice this debacle until half an hour later. By the time I went back to retrieve my furniture, there was a family of lizards living in my couch and loveseat, which now had no legs.

Mark and I move into our apartment with our low riding lizard furniture. A couple days go by before we get a knock at the door. We don't know who our roommates are going to be. We open the door, and Walla! It's the guy I stole the ball from 2 years prior in the biggest game of my High School career, and his teammate, who guarded Mark like a Hawk the entire game. You could not have possibly drawn up a more awkward situation. Especially since during the summer leading up to this, the sister of the guy I stole the ball from slapped me in the face at an 18 and over club because I apparently "ruined her brother's life."

Needless to say, I only lasted a few months. I actually became good friends with both my new roommates, but the toll of practice and school were too much. I was literally flunking out of school. When I say "literally", I mean, I was literally flunking out of school. If my memory serves me correct, I had a .5 GPA. In case you didn't notice, there weren't any other numbers in front of the decimal.

One afternoon, I finally just packed up the old Plymouth Laser and moved back home to Sevierville. I stayed in school, went back to work at The Rhythm Section in Gatlinburg (an incredible record store that I had been working at since I was 14), and tried to reevaluate my life. Ok, let me rephrase that. I quit playing basketball, went back to work at a really cool job with my best friends, and we decided to go with a techno/grunge lifestyle.

I quickly went from a short haired basketball player to a "bangs down to my chest, slam dancing, grunge and techno listening, fun loving, carefree young man" at the Underground Dance Club in Knoxville, 3 to 4 nights a week. DJ Storm was my life now. I really can't explain how it happened. It was a quick transition. My life was taking a turn, and a sudden one at that. Now, I didn't get into any trouble. I stayed grounded. But, I was loving life and letting go a bit. My 2 best friends were at my side the entire time, and it was by far one of the best times of my life.

I then transferred to the University of Tennessee, majoring in "I still have no clue." That whole aspiration thing still hadn't sunk in. I really had no idea what I wanted to do. I was infatuated with going to the Underground, playing basketball in Men's leagues in Sevierville and Gatlinburg, and listening to good music. That was about it.

Then, my life took another turn. At age 22, I got married. A year later, my son Weston was born. At this point, I was only a junior in college (hence the title of this section, The Many, Many College Years.)

I was already done with the partying at this point. However, I was still pretty much just a college kid with no direction, who happened to be married with a child. I didn't have a single aspiration in life, except maybe playing professional basketball in Europe. For several months, I was convinced that that was what I was going to do. Obviously, that never happened.

Weston and I when he was a little guy. I can't believe he is 19 now. I also can't believe there was a time when I didn't have facial hair.

I quickly realized that I needed to hurry up and finish school and get a real job. What that would be? I had no idea. I was a junior in college, taking my son to Chaucer class with me (I had a really cool professor who loved the fact that I also collected rare books), and I was finally making good grades again. I had to. I was a dad. I had responsibilities. I just wasn't sure how to be responsible yet.

As my Senior year rolled around, there was an actual "degree" in sight. Bachelor of Arts in English, specifically Literature. More specifically, Medieval Literature. The only reason for this was that I had taken the most credits in this concentration, so I just went with it. I already knew at this point that playing in Men's league basketball wasn't going to pay any bills, and that a "real" job was on its way. What "it" was scared the hell out of me.

As graduation neared, I went to a job fair for people like me. The people with no aspirations that were getting a degree in something they didn't really mean to get. This is where my life would change in a drastic way. I didn't know it at the time, but this would consume the next 14 years of my life.

The Professional Life

At this job fair, I met a guy named Bill Freeman. Still friends to this day, Bill convinced me to come in for an interview with American Express Financial Advisors. I know what you are thinking. Completely natural transition from Literature to Financial Services. Yeah.

I'm going to condense these next 14 years. It's still a blur. The following will be a series of short sentences and paragraphs.

I spent a year at American Express. I then got a job at a major regional bank as a broker and financial planner, where I would also learn to appreciate charitable work.

After 7 years of this, I got divorced.

Then, I got married again. A year later, I had another son, Hudson.

Weston and Hudson, wearing nice clothes and not fighting. Rare picture.

After Hudson was born, things went nuts. We owned a business for a year, it didn't last, I went to another bank, and then got divorced again after 7 years.

I spent 3 years at that second bank, before I would go on to spend 3 more years at a third bank.

A total of 14 years as a financial advisor, with over a dozen licenses. 2 divorces. 2 wonderful boys.

14 years would normally sound like a long time, but in my case, it was a quick whirlwind.

Where this life would lead me next.....nobody saw it coming.

Hudson and I at his field day.

The First Open Mic

Background

It was early February, 2010. I was getting separated, with divorce foreseeably imminent. I was losing my house, a large one at that, due to financial difficulties. Everything was a mess. I wasn't really sure what to do at this point. I knew I was getting ready to move, but to where, I had no idea. I knew I was about to be a single dad, for the second time, and I wasn't exactly sure how to handle it.

Obviously, when you are getting divorced for a second time, you begin to question everything. You try to figure out what is wrong. You start to reevaluate your life, yourself, your purpose. Nothing seems real, there is a lot of self-doubt, and anger. Most of all, though, it is primarily confusion that consumes you.

Even before all of this, I already hated being an investment broker. Every second of it. It just wasn't me. However, it was a means to make money. I was fairly good at it, though if I knew then what I know now, I could have been great at it. I just didn't have the drive, the love, or the motivation to be the best. I just did what I had to do to make money and survive.

I was 36 years old, so I had basically given up on my dream of being a High School or College basketball coach. Trust me, on an annual basis since the age of 23, I had researched the rules and what I would need to do as far as education to become a coach. And, every year, I decided it was both too much work and would interfere with me making money for the family.

I had created an internal laziness and lack of drive over the years. I just assumed I was destined to work a regular job just like everyone else. I was approaching 40, with kids, so I thought that being "normal" was my lifelong path. Not that there is anything wrong with being normal.

Being funny was just a characteristic I had possessed since I was a kid. Around my friends, coworkers, teammates, or whoever was in the vicinity, I always found joy in making people laugh. I never had any inkling of a thought about doing anything productive with my sense of humor. Instead, I just cracked stupid jokes all day, waiting for the laughter. It was enough.

The Week Before

So, it's February 10, 2010. I was 36 years old. I had never been to a stand-up comedy show in my life. Not an open mic, a show at a comedy club, or a theater. Matter of fact, I had just recently found out there was a comedy club in Knoxville, not too far from my house. Now, I know this sounds weird. It sounds weird to me now, that's for sure. Man, life can be so strange sometimes.

Up until this day, my only experience with stand-up comedy was watching it on TV. That's it. I watched it every chance I could, however it was not like I watch it now. No, at that time, I was just an audience member. I enjoyed just "laughing" at the comics. It's not like that anymore. Now I'm analytical, picking apart technical deficiencies and breaking down every bit and joke I hear. Honestly, I like the old way better.

For a reason that I can't remember, I ended up going to Side Splitters Comedy Club in Knoxville on Wednesday, February 10th, 2010 to watch the open mic. All I remember is things weren't great at home, I needed something to do to keep my mind off things, and apparently this is what it was, and effectively how it all started.

I didn't know how comedy clubs worked. I didn't know what to expect. There I was, a 36 year old father of 2, investment broker, nervous, unsure of everything in my own life, and about to walk into this place for the first time, completely uncertain of what I would find inside the door.

The recently closed Side Splitters Comedy Club in West Knoxville. Incredible amount of memories lie in this ghostly picture now.

So, I pull my KIA into the parking lot, which is full of strangely placed potholes. I'm debating on whether or not to stay. Little did I know at the time, but I would be debating whether or not to go in almost on a weekly basis for a long time to come.

Finally, I get up the nerve and tell myself "What is the worst that's going to happen? You going to laugh yourself to death?" I wasn't even performing. I was just there to watch. Yet I had this uneasy feeling. Like there was pressure on me to do something. Thinking back, it's almost as if my subconscious was telling me that I was about to change my entire life over the next couple of hours.

I get out of the KIA, which would also become well known around this building in the near future. My next move was one that I would watch hundreds, maybe closer to a thousand spectators do over the next few years. I walked up to the false door, only to hear an open micer who was smoking outside say "hey man...wrong door." Great, I'm already an idiot.

Once I actually get through the "real" door, I find myself standing in a small room with a bar. To my right, just inside the door, is a ticket booth, where I am told it's $10.00 for admission, but that includes a drink of my choice and pizza. So, I'm already thinking this was a good idea.

There are people sitting at the bar, at long tables, and in random chairs scattered around in this small room. They are all facing a very small stage with a microphone and stand. There are pictures of famous comedians all over the room. It's quite intimidating. If you would have told me that night that I would have an entire corner of pictures and articles on that wall of myself in the near future, I would have laughed.

Now, remember, this is all new to me. I'd seen many stand-up comedy specials on TV, but never something this small in such an intimate setting, or in person. I was nervous for whoever was about to attempt this. It seemed like a crazy idea to me. However, I was excited to see how this was going to play out.

I grab a seat at the bar, hand the bartender my ticket, and order a drink. I gaze around the room, only to see a plethora of interesting looking characters. I don't know who any of these people are. I don't know if they are comedians or audience members such as myself. They mostly seem to be in groups, and younger than me. There are a few older straggly looking guys here and there frantically looking at pieces of paper. That's the room. That's where I was on a Wednesday in February.

Then, in an instant, half of the room just leaves. They go into another room with double doors. I tried to peek in there from the bar, but all I could see were more tables. Aha! This was the room where the fake doors led. I still didn't know exactly what that room was, but I was definitely intrigued.

At this point, it's about 20 minutes until the open mic is supposed to start. I just sit there. I'm looking at the pictures on the wall of the famous comedians. I was thinking "What an interesting life. Telling jokes and making money. I wonder how they started doing something like this? I wonder if they have classes or something? Seems interesting." No joke, these were the types of things going through my head. I had actually forgotten about the open mic. Instead, I was fascinated with the professional comedians on the wall. Many of them I had seen on TV, either in sitcoms or Stand Up specials.

Now, when I say fascinated, I don't mean that I was remotely even contemplating giving it a try. I was just curious. I didn't come here to start something new. I came here to get of the house and experience something new. That was it. Pretty simple.

Next thing I know, all the people who had previously left come back through the double doors. Some are excited, some are nervous, some are just there. About 5 minutes go by, the lights go off in this tiny room, and it's show time.

The show begins with a guy happily jogging up to the stage. He fumbles the mic for a bit, then welcomes everyone, stating that he will be our host for the evening. He says that we will be hearing many funny comedians tonight. I can't remember the number exactly, but it was in the teens. He asks that we be as quiet as possible, tip the wait staff, and have fun. Sounds easy enough.

After his announcements, he begins to tell jokes. I was confused. He was the host. I thought he was just going to be introducing people and giving us the guidelines? I had no idea he was supposed to be funny too.

It didn't take long to notice that he wasn't really trying too hard to be funny. It would be later down the road that I would learn why this was. He did a few minutes of short, clean jokes. Then he introduced the first comic. At this point, I was captivated. In just a few short minutes, I had gone from fascination and intrigue to "This is not what I thought it would be. This is amazing."

Over the next couple of hours, I sat and watched comic after comic let it go. Men and women. Clean and dirty. And Nasty. Anything and everything. Some were polished, some were shaking. Some were happy to be there. Some were just going through the motions. I started timing them. I determined they were each getting 5 to 6 minutes each. It was one of the most interesting nights of my life. Yet, I still didn't picture myself doing anything like this. It was intriguing, that was all.

At the end of the show, the host gave a few more announcements. Tip the bartender, drive safe, etc. One of his announcements, however, was that if anyone was interested in trying stand-up at the next open mic, they could see them afterwards or visit the website.

The lights came on. Everyone seemed happy. They were congratulating each other, talking about certain jokes. Friends and fans were overly gracious with their praises to the person they were there to see. It was a weird feeling. Since I didn't know anyone, I was like the creepy loner guy just watching from a far. I finally decided to leave. On my way out, they thanked me, and I saw a sign-up sheet for the next open mic. For a split second, I thought "Should I? I'm pretty funny, I think."

Instead, I walked through the door, got in my car, and drove back home to my kids. Normally, at this time of night on a Wednesday, I was thinking about what bank I was scheduled to be at the next morning, or what appointments I had. Not this time. With my life already in a flux due to the upcoming divorce, and knowing that things were about to change dramatically, I let my brain drift into a crazy dream world where I was the one telling jokes on that tiny little stage.

I specifically remember pulling into the driveway that night, parking my car, turning off the lights, and just sitting there in the dark. I thought to myself "Could I do it? Should I try it? Just once? It seemed like fun? I could use a distraction. Yeah. Let's try it. Just once though, then back to my normal, screwed up, messed up life."

During this time, I was working for a bank in Sevierville and Seymour, Tennessee. It was roughly 40 minutes from where I lived in Knoxville. My boss, Bryan Lawson, and I had become good friends, traveling together, going to 2 and 3 day seminars, talking on the phone daily, etc. By far the coolest boss I ever had during my long banking and investment career, and someone I still consider a close friend to this day.

The reason I bring up Bryan is that he, in simplest terms, encouraged me to give stand-up a try. Matter of fact, if it wasn't for his knowledge of stand-up comedy in general, and his sense of humor being so much like mine, I would probably have never even considered going to watch that first open mic to begin with.

So, that next morning I went into my office. I called Bryan, and told him about the open mic I had watched the night before. We talked about it for a while, with me telling him some of the stuff I had heard, the interesting characters that I saw, and the experience in general. I should have known he was going to encourage me to give it a try myself. I should have known.

The next day, I sent the email to sign up for the next open mic at Side Splitters Comedy Club. The email that would change my life forever, or at least up until me writing this. Sorry, I don't know the future yet.

Show Time 02/17/2010

A few days before, I had sent an email to Side Splitters to sign up for the following week's open mic. No joke, by far the most difficult and terrifying email I've ever sent.

After getting a reply back stating that I was on the list, my excitement quickly turned into fear. What had I done? I was a 36 year old, soon to be single father of 2 boys, investment banker. I had no business signing up for an open mic comedy night!

I must have read over the guidelines 100 times. I had 6 minutes. Check. I can say whatever I want. Check. Don't go over 6 minutes, or they will play music and cut the microphone off. Check. If they play music, then I will not be able to come back. Check. Be there by 7:30 for the 8:00 show. Check.

My next move? Yeah, you guessed it. Call Bryan. I'm pretty sure the conversation went like this "Hey...ummm....soooooo.....I signed up for the open mic. I have 6 minutes. That's it. Sooooo....ummmmmm.....what do I do now?"

At this point I only had 5 days to prepare. I know it doesn't sound like that difficult of a scenario. 6 minutes of jokes in 5 days. But, let me tell you, I was literally in physical pain. The nerves were overwhelming. I had seen a little over a dozen people attempt it the week before, and that was enough. I saw professionals bomb that night. I saw first timers bomb. I was 36 years old, competitive by nature, I had a career. I wasn't prepared to bomb.

I spent the next 5 days writing. Bryan and I wrote stuff over the phone. He was in Virginia, so it wasn't like we could just sit down over lunch. No, we had to wing this thing over the phone. I was not confident.

The day of the open mic, I was 100% ready...to back out. I had the feeling of throwing up in my mouth all day. Just being honest here. Yeah, I had memorized my 6 minutes. However, I didn't think any of it was funny anymore. Matter of fact, every time I practiced it in the mirror, it just sounded more and more stupid. My new found bucket list item was about to go down in the worst way imaginable. I just knew it.

I also had a lot of support from my next door neighbor, Jason. He either thought I was a funny neighbor, or just felt sorry for me. I don't know. Either way, thankfully, he decided to come watch me that first night. Then, at the last minute, my 2 best friends from High School and College said they were coming. Great. The pressure was on.

I pull into the pot hole filled parking lot at Side Splitters, about 3 hours early. Another habit I would keep going for several months to come. There are hardly any cars there. I sit. I pull out my piece of paper, with scribbled jokes that I had been working on for the last 5 days. I question them all. I don't think they are funny anymore. I contemplate leaving. I almost throw up. Then I start laughing and think "What's the worst that could happen?" Then I want to throw up again. This would go on for an hour.

Finally, I go in to the tiny side lounge, bar thingy. For some reason, the stage looks even smaller than it did the week prior, when I was a spectator. Everything seemed smaller. And scarier. I honestly can't recall being that petrified in my entire life. I just wanted to get this over with, go home, sleep, and get back to my boring banking life.

There weren't too many people in there at that time. It's still about an hour before the show is supposed to begin, so I pay my $10 at the ticket counter (yes, as a performer you still had to pay, and yes, a lot of other comics complained about this.) Now, I have a free drink ticket in my hand. Should I save it for later? Ummm, yeah, no. I needed it right then. My nerves were shot. People were staring at me. They could obviously sense the fear in me, and the notebook in my hand was visibly shaking, rattling the pages.

The bartender was Rusty Penland. I'm sure if you asked him today he would remember the fear in my eyes that night. He talked to me for a while and tried to help calm me down. Rusty and I would become very close friends after that night, and it's a friendship that I still hold very close to this day. He was also one of my biggest critics, and would be one of the first people I would ask "how was it?" after each set. I'd love for him to see me perform now. It's been years.

People began to pile into this small room. It started to feel like a fun house at the fair, with the walls contracting and scary faces yelling at me. I had never been one to back out of something, but I was seriously contemplating it at this point.

Around 7:30, with the show set to start at 8, all the comics are called over the microphone from the ticket booth to head to the "main showroom." I have no clue where that is, so I start to follow all the other people with notebooks. They head for the double doors that I had seen the week before. Finally, I know what that room is.

We get in there, and everyone sits on the top level at small tables covered in pencils and comment cards. I do a quick scan of the room. There are many, many tables, and a bigger stage with a microphone, a stool, and a big screen rolled up above. A sign behind the stage says "Side Splitters Comedy Club." Now. Now I had seen my first comedy club in person. It was, to say the least, extremely intimidating. I was nervous, and at that point had no intentions of ever even sitting close to that stage, much less performing on it. Just a scared 36 year old dad for no reason.

The meeting starts, and the club managers begin laying the ground rules for the upcoming show. Most everyone in the room knew each other. There were a few new people, like myself, who got introduced to everyone else. We are told to write our names and a short intro on the comment cards on the table. This is when things got real.

The realization that someone else was going to say my name, out loud, to other people was slowly and painfully sinking in. I thought about saying I had to use the restroom, chalking up the night to only getting to use a free drink ticket, and bolting. Instead, I told myself that this was a one-time thing, that I had worked hard on writing jokes, and that I just needed to get this over with. I told myself "It's not like any of these people will ever see you again, so just do it."

I write my intro. I honestly don't remember what I wrote. It was probably something like "Hi. My name is Alex." Who knows. The next thing I know, they are saying that whoever got there first gets to pick their spot first, whoever got there last has to go first, and that they will then place the rest of us by asking us, in the order we arrived, where we would like. Well, I was there 3 hours early. In the parking lot. If I would have known that by telling them I was there earlier I could pick any spot I wanted, I would have checked in first instead of sitting in my car, false alarm throwing up every 30 seconds. At least I wasn't last.

As I recall, I got to go somewhere in the middle, like 12th. I was ok with that. It would give me time to keep memorizing my terrible jokes, watch the others, and see what the crowd was like. Not that it would matter, but that's what I kept telling myself.

We then turned in our intro cards, everyone started talking to each other, and we walked back into the lounge. Some of the comics started talking to me, asking where I was from, etc. I think they could tell I was terrified, so they were trying to help calm me down. For about 9 steps, it worked. Then, the doors swung open, I saw more people gathered in the tiny room, including my next door neighbor and my 2 best friends from High School and College. I had never fainted before, but it crossed my mind to do it then.

There is literally 5 minutes left before the Emcee takes the stage to kick things off. I'm in the back corner, pacing, trying to do math. Emcee, 5 minutes. 11 comics, 6 minutes. Emcee introducing each comic, probably 1 minute max. So, how much time before I have to do this? Someone! Please! Get me a calculator and an airline puke bag! Where's the bathroom?! Why am I here?! What is going on!? How did this happen?! Ugh!!!

The lights go off. The manager announces the show is starting from the booth. The Emcee takes the stage. This is it.

I don't even know what happened next. I had calculated 11 other comics doing 6 minutes each before me, plus all the Emcee stuff. Next thing I know, I hear my name called to come to the stage. I didn't even hear my intro. I was numb.

At this point in my life, the only time I had ever handled a microphone was when I was 20 years old and in a garage grunge band that never even played a show, and at podiums doing seminars from my investment banking career. That was it. So, naturally, I had no clue what to do with the mic.

After fumbling with the mic for about 30 seconds, I sputter out my first joke:

"Hi. You might recognize me from being on stage before. Yeah, I was the guy wearing a bowtie, thong, and covered in baby oil."

That. Was. It.

Who would have ever thought that that joke would transform into a closer in major comedy clubs in the years to come? Well, it did. Sorry, I'm jumping ahead a bit. Let's get back to this night.

After that first joke, I honestly can't remember what I said next. I even have a video from that first night sitting right here next to me on the desk. I still haven't watched it, almost 6 years later.

Now, remember earlier when I said that I had received an email telling me the rules? I only had 6 minutes, and if I went over the 6 minutes, they would play music signaling for me to get off the stage and to never come back. Remember that rule?

Well, yeah, that happened. Not only did the music come on, but I kept talking over the music. The Emcee literally had to come get me off the stage. I was rambling. About nothing, I'm sure.

I walked off the stage, embarrassed, and sat in the corner. On the one hand, I was relieved it was over, and that I could go back to my boring life of being an investment banker. On the other hand, I had never felt so much exhilaration and excitement, except maybe a High School basketball game in front of thousands of people 18 years before. I was conflicted inside. I knew that I wanted to do it again, but I also knew that I would never be allowed back because I didn't follow the rules.

My first night onstage. February 17, 2010. A bit blurry, yes. I think my nerves were shaking the camera in the back of the room.

My friends were encouraging me. They told me I did great. I was confused. We had been best friends since we were in High School. They knew me better than anyone. I wasn't even supposed to be the funny one of the group. Yet, here I was, at a comedy club telling jokes to strangers 20 years later. If you are someone like me, who likes to use the phrase "that was surreal!", then that was definitely the most "surreal" moment of my life at that point.

My next door neighbor, Jason, was positive as well. We had become very close friends over the previous few years, and spent a lot of time joking around. We had the same sense of humor. It was nice to have tried something new like this, and have the people closest to me tell me I did well. At that point in my life, I needed it.

Finally, a couple hours after it began, the show ended. The lights came on. Like I had seen the week before, people began to scatter. They were talking, congratulating each other. Fans and friends were telling random comics how funny they were. I had my friends, I was happy. Then, the moment of truth walked towards me. The club manager, Bridgette.

I was expecting a "Thanks for coming. Sorry you went over your time and didn't follow the rules. Please, feel free to come watch another show some time and support local comedy." However, the opposite happened.

She came up and said "Hey. Thanks for coming. You did really well for your first time! I know you went over your time, but you have potential. Please, feel free to sign up and come back next week!"

What. Just. Happened.

I paid my tab. I'm pretty sure I owed more than the free drink ticket at this point. I told my friends bye. I walked, briskly and completely frozen to my KIA, that was now sitting alone in between the 2 biggest potholes in the parking lot. Yes, I may have been one of the first ones to arrive earlier, but apparently my nerves caused me to pick the worst space in the lot.

I put the keys in the ignition. I sat. I stared at the scary motel next door. I thought to myself:

What. Just. Happened.

I drove home. 10 minute drive that felt like 2 hours. My emotions scaled the entire spectrum. I wasn't really sure what to think at this point. I knew, without a doubt, that I had just embarked upon the most exciting night of my life. I also knew, however, that it was an unrealistic feeling that would soon be crushed. It was a short, 10 minute battle, between bucket list item and "this is what I want to do now" kind of thing.

So, I went home, got in bed, came back to reality, and closed my eyes with an unsatisfied frown on my face.

I would wake up the next morning, though, with an optimistic smile on my face.

The First Year

The Day After The First Night

I woke up. I was confused. The night before was a blur. No, I wasn't hungover or anything like that. I was just coming off one of the most emotional rollercoasters of my life. What a crazy 24 hours! I had to think about this. What's my next move? Just forget about it and move on? Pursue it? Pursue it?!!! Am I an idiot? Pursue what? I did an open mic. I messed it up, big time. It was a simple decision, really.

Pursue it.

I went into the office. 45 minute drive. Great, more time to reflect on the night before. I got to the office. I looked at clients' accounts. I made sure everything was in order. No problems. Check. Call Bryan.

"Dude....It was amazing." Those were probably the first words out of my mouth. "I did those jokes we wrote together, people actually laughed, the manager told me I did great for my first time. Oh, and I went over the 6 minutes but no big deal." I'm pretty sure that's what I said next.

After discussing all the details, I sent a second email to Side Splitters, signing up for the next week's open mic. I was too excited not to.

The days leading up to the next open mic would probably be, I must say, the dumbest days in comedy I've had yet.

The Second Open Mic

I don't really know how this happened. Somehow, Bryan and I started talking about a Hand Turkey. You know, the kind you outline with your hand when you are 5 years old. Next thing I know, we had both convinced ourselves that I should do one long, 6 minute joke, for my next open mic, about Hand Turkeys.

To say I was overconfident from that first open mic would be an understatement. To say I was a complete moron to think that I could just do one long bit about hand turkeys would be an even bigger understatement. Unfortunately, I didn't have the above 2 statements to work with 5 years ago.

The second open mic rolls around a week later. I'm super confident. I'm excited. I feel like a veteran of comedy. I am literally this close to a one hour TV special. I am the man. I'm doing the Hand Turkey bit. It will kill.

Oh, it killed alright. It killed the entire show. It killed my confidence. It killed everything in sight. It was so bad, that not only did I contemplate not doing comedy ever again, but I thought I needed to move to another city. It was that bad.

Apparently, as I would soon learn, you are not supposed to do one long joke, especially 6 minutes long, with the only punchline being at the end.

I would skip the next open mic. I was humiliated. I was convinced that I only had one good night in me. My original thought was correct, it was a bucket list thing. I did it. Move on.

Bryan stayed on me though. My best friends from High School encouraged me to keep trying. My neighbor, Jason, said don't give up yet. My parents said to just do it. That was all I needed. I had amazing support through a rough time in my life. I really needed an out. My basketball career had ended years before. Besides the days I had my kids, this was all I had now to look forward to.

The Next 11 Months

After a couple weeks, I went back. I regrouped. Bryan and I wrote jokes over the phone. We tried to fix some of the ones I did that first night. Made them better. I started to make friends at Side Splitters. With the comics, the bartenders, the wait staff, the managers. Things were falling into place. I had something, besides spending time with my kids, to look forward to now.

8 months into comedy. Sharing the stage, in the Rocky Top Comedy Contest, with some amazing comics. I'm the 3rd from the right.

I moved out of the house and into a condo/townhouse, only a mile away from Side Splitters. Looking back at it now, I wonder if it was a subconscious decision to move there. At the time, I was only thinking of the kid's school situation.

I had 50% custody of the kids, and it was a situation where every week rotated. My relationships with their mothers were good, and they were understanding that I needed do these open mics, even if to just keep me distracted. So, I had a very flexible schedule with the boys.

I was beginning to feel very comfortable at the club. On a weekly basis, I was meeting new comics from Chattanooga, Nashville, Kentucky, Atlanta, Asheville, and other cities from around the Southeast. Regionally, it was a very popular and sought after open mic to be on.

I knew, however, that this couldn't just be a hobby. I was too busy in real life to just treat this like a side thing. I had a full time job, a lot of driving on a daily basis, and kids. I had too many responsibilities to dedicate so much time to something that was just for fun.

Being a little older than many of the comics, and with all of the added responsibilities, I made a decision pretty early on to just go for it, give it everything I had, learn all the ins and outs, and do whatever possible to make myself better every time I hit the stage.

During that first year there would many incredible events that would all come together, leading my life on a path that I never saw coming. It started as a whimsical joke, then became a crazy dream, only to develop into something I couldn't imagine stopping, ever.

That first year. What a year. I would meet many new, incredible people. I would win a few contests. I would make my way into that mystical showroom, on the big stage. Most importantly, though, I would make friends with 2 of the most influential people in my life, permanently changing the course of my existence.

What a first year.

Doing It My Way

A Little Background

So, remember when I said in the introduction that I may jump around a little bit to keep things interesting? Well, here we go.

Now, I'm not a legend of comedy. I'm not a guy who's on TV. I'm not a household name. I'm not claiming to have all of the answers, or any of the answers for that matter. I have perspective based on what I've been through. That's it. Don't take this as fact, or even as an industry based opinion. This is just MY perspective, based upon MY own experiences.

With that being said, as a mature and intelligent person (once again, opinion), I have delved into many different domains of the comedy world. The traditional comedy clubs, the underground bar shows, regular bar shows, open mics, charity events, theaters, corporate events, contests, festivals, and shows that you just can't categorize. I have experienced all of these, in 5 short years, as a headliner, a middle or feature, and as a host. I have done an hour PG and R rated, multiple times. So, my experience, although in a short amount of time, has been fairly broad.

Hosting at Side Splitters. Doing the dirty work, clean.

You all probably know this already, but, just in case, here is a quick refresher. I won't dedicate more than this paragraph to this subject. There are basically 4 different types of spots for shows. Not every show has all of these, either. It can vary. These are just the basics. You have your host, or emcee, who is responsible for getting the show started and introducing the comics, and making announcements. Sometimes the host is required to be clean, sometimes not. Just depends on the venue. You sometimes have a guest spot, someone who is more than likely not getting paid, but gets an opportunity to do a few minutes to showcase their ability. Then there is the feature, or middle. This is an experienced comic who can easily do 20-30 minutes, and is the main warm up for the headliner. The headliner is exactly what it sounds like. The main comic everyone came to see. Typically 45 minutes to an hour. This is what every comic strives to be, hopefully.

As far as specific shows go, I will go into detail on those later. The second half of the book is dedicated to stories from all types of venues and events. For now, though, I just want to give you a glimpse of my situation.

My progression over the last 5 years has, on the one hand, been steady. On the other hand, it's been sporadic. That is why it's tough to categorize me as a comedian. On a local level, this works out great for me. I can get booked for virtually any type of show, in any venue, for any crowd. On a broader, national level, this would be my downfall.

I made a decision during that first year to go against the norm, and make myself a well-rounded comic. The jury is still out on whether or not that was a good decision.

What Am I?

This is a question I ask myself every day. Where do I belong in the world of stand-up comedy? What is my role? What am I best at? I have been successful in comedy clubs. I have been successful in bars. I have been successful doing charity, corporate, and out of the norm events. I have won contests. I have enjoyed and been just as entertaining to a crowd doing an hour PG as I have R. I've made money. I've worked for free. I've bombed doing PG. I've bombed doing R. I've performed in a theater for over 1,000 people. I've performed in an Alley for 7 people.

Where do I go? What am I supposed to do? How am I supposed to pursue this? Am I supposed to just hit the road and work clubs 4 nights a week like everyone says I should? Should I just tour, working underground bar shows to packed crowds making $100 a night but having fun? Should I focus more on corporate shows and make a lot of money while limiting myself comedically?

For a majority of comics, they pick one of the above and go with it. It makes sense. Do what you are BEST at. This is the best way to be successful, get on TV, headline comedy clubs and theaters, or whatever it is they want to achieve. For me, though, it's different.

I love making people laugh. Period. I love being on a stage, no matter what the venue is, and seeing the audience having fun. More importantly, though, I love my family. My wife, my kids. I love spending time with them. If I'm going to be successful, it's going to be on my own terms. It's going to work around my family's schedule, not my own personal longing of making people laugh.

This isn't for everyone. I have many friends who are comics, or musicians, or any other type of artist who do a great job of balancing both their work and family. Honestly, I haven't found the best way to balance it yet. I'm still in the trial phase.

How Did I Get Like This?

The best way to answer this, simply, is to just give you a brief timeline of my progression as a comic. It didn't happen naturally. It was a random event that took me one place or another. It was a split decision here or there that made me deviate from what I was already doing. The best way to put it, honestly, is that I have no clue. It just keeps evolving.

Obviously, it all started with open mics at Side Splitters. Week after week, writing new material, mostly R rated, to appease the crowd. 6 minutes every week. That's all I needed. It sounds easy, but it's not. Once I figured out what I was supposed to be doing (A single 6 minute joke about a Hand Turkey is not it), I began honing my craft, making the decent jokes better, the good jokes great. It wasn't about writing an entire new 6 minutes every week. It was about being better, funnier, and developing each area of being a good comic, one little step at a time. Work on my writing, my timing, my stage presence, my facial expressions, my style. It's not just as simple as writing good material. There is so much more to it.

Pretty early on, I won back to back contests. I was on cloud 9. I had already been humiliated, so I knew how that felt. Winning these contests didn't give me a big head. I just expected it at this point. I knew I had outworked everyone else, and that's the way it was supposed to be. If I didn't have the kids, I was there on the weekends, watching the nationally touring headliners, every show, do their thing. I paid attention. I listened to the club owners and managers. I was older. I was focused.

I started traveling, doing open mics in other cities. Comedy clubs, bars, wherever. I teamed up with a couple of mentors, that you will learn about soon enough, and soaked it all in. I was getting better and better with every touch of the mic thanks to them.

This hard work started to pay off very quickly. I was all over the place. We started our own open mic in a bar, I was getting invited to festivals, I was touring the country, and of course, I was working my way up the ladder at Side Splitters.

A little over 6 months in at Side Splitters, as an open mic comic and a host of the open mics, I got my first chance at a guest spot in the main showroom, for a nationally touring headliner, James Johann. This is where I would get my first "real" taste of what stand-up comedy was like. Oh, and yeah, I loved it.

After that, I would start getting more offers for more shows. One of importance, in my second year, would be as the primary entertainment for my 20 year High School Reunion. This would be my first taste of PG comedy. A couple months later, I would be asked to feature for a huge New Year's Eve show in downtown Knoxville, with over 450 in attendance, including children. Also PG, obviously. In just a few months, my focus went from 6 to 10 minute R rated sets to 25 to 45 minute PG sets. It was unexpected, unplanned, and scary. However, I loved it just as much.

Those first 2 years were wild. I would also start my own show in Sevierville, TN, and headline it. 1 hour sets, R rated. I was going full steam ahead, in every direction. Charity events at the Comedy Catch in Chattanooga, festivals, Side Splitters, bar shows, my own show. All while spending every second with my kids when they were with me, coaching their basketball teams, going to their school events. Working at the bank. Driving all the time. It was a crazy time, but well worth it.

Right at my 2 year anniversary from that first open mic, my life would change again. I would meet the love of my life, and her kids. My direction would shift again.

The next 3 years would see me change focus. The first 2 years, it was about me and my pursuit of comedy half of the time, my kids the other half. If I didn't have the boys with me, I was doing shows somewhere. When I had the boys, I was with them.

Now, it was all changing. My focus was on Jenny and all 4 boys! Luckily, she's been the biggest supporter of my quest to make it in this business. She would push me to book shows I normally wouldn't. She would go with me, sitting in the crowd encouraging me, laughing, promoting, managing the non-comedy part. She has always been there for me, through the good times and the bad, the good shows and the horrible, as you will soon read about.

Due to many circumstances, I would start booking shows in areas that I was previously unfamiliar with. Headlining bar shows in states far away, corporate shows to make money for the family, anything and everything I could. You name it, Jenny and I were there, as long as it fit our family's calendar. For the record, our calendar involves 5 families due to 3 combined divorces, and then our own families, including grandparents and extended family in multiple states, etc. It's not the easiest schedule to work with, I promise you.

All in all, these first 5 years of stand-up comedy have been incredible. I've been extremely lucky to have had the opportunities that I've been afforded. Yes, I've worked hard at it, but it's not always that easy. There has been a lot of luck involved. Being in the right place at the right time. Meeting the right people. Having unbelievable support from every angle. Not everyone gets as lucky as I have, and I know it. I don't take it for granted. I feel fortunate to have so many great friends and a family that supports me.

M.L.C. Comedians

I could write an entire book on this part of my life. To be honest, I don't really even know where to start. It's going to be a long chapter folks.

Remember, a couple of chapters before, where I said I met 2 of the most influential people in my life? Well, this is it. I specifically didn't mention them before now. They deserve their own special attention.

The Beginning

In early 2010, after several weeks of doing open mics at Side Splitters Comedy Club, something happened.

Up until now, I only had one real friend there at the open mics. Dave Wright. We had become friends pretty quickly. Dave was fairly edgy, as was I in the beginning. We were a little bit older than most of the guys, and we just hit it off. We would meet for dinner before the shows, go over our sets, and just hang out.

One Wednesday evening, as usual, all the comics were standing in line outside to get in for the show. I was standing behind a guy that I had seen before, but not yet talked to. I listened as he entertained the entire line, talking about his saltwater pool. Everybody was dying laughing. I don't even remember what he said, I just remember that I was thinking "this guy is hilarious."

He was a few years older than me, but not by much. He had his own style. The sportcoat, jeans, and snakeskin boots. The confidence. The swagger. The "I'm gonna kill it. I don't have a piece of paper with my jokes written down like all of you idiots" swagger. He was different. I wanted to be his friend.

This was Jay Pinkerton.

Not long after that, I would notice another guy. This guy was respected by everyone. He had been around the block. He had been doing comedy for years, took some time off, then came back. He had a completely different style than everyone else. He was the king of the one liners. He wasn't as approachable as Jay, however. To be honest, I was a little intimidated.

This was Sandy Goddard.

Over the next few weeks, I would start hanging around these guys. I would interject myself into conversations with them. As soon as the light would come on after the open mic, I would rush over to where they were. I wanted to learn from them. That was it. I never expected what was to become of those odd confrontations.

How The M.L.C. Began

This part is kind of groggy. I honestly don't know, exactly, how it began. Dave and I had become good friends. Jay and I had become good friends. We all looked up to Sandy, who had experience, had traveled and had connections at other venues, and wanted to do what he was doing.

One night after an open mic at Side Splitters, literally a couple months after I had even just begun doing this whole thing, the 4 of us were standing outside. We started talking. The next thing I knew, we had planned a trip to Asheville, NC. The 4 of us were going to go do an open mic at The Hangar. Needless to say, I was a nervous wreck. I was about to embark upon a trip to another venue for the first time. I still wasn't comfortable telling jokes in front of the crowd I knew in Knoxville, much less a new crowd in another state.

The time comes. The 4 of us hop in the car and head to Asheville. I think we were funnier that night on the car ride there than we ended up being at the show. We were having a blast, but I was seriously trying to hide my nervousness. I was hoping for one of those historical random Asheville mountain rock slides to block our way. Unfortunately, that didn't happen, and we show up to the venue. At an Airport.

We walk in, I'm shaking. All the confidence I had built up over the first couple of months was still sitting outside in Jay's car. I'm pretty sure it stayed there all night.

We pass by several groups of people sitting at tables. Apparently, these were people having cocktails while waiting on their flights, who inadvertently became audience members. Small airport, I'm telling you.

We introduce ourselves as the guys from Knoxville. They were very welcoming. We grabbed a table as far from the stage as possible, which was basically just the floor, in order to evaluate our surroundings.

When the show began, we quickly realized it was more like a circle type setting and poetry reading. It was still technically stand-up comedy, but it was unlike anything any of us had ever seen, even Sandy. It was pretty scary.

There were probably 20 comics there that night. The 4 of us were sprinkled among the line-up. It didn't take long to figure out 2 things: Number 1, the other comics were intelligent, English Major type comics. Number 2, the audience that consisted of people awaiting their flights, hated to laugh.

However, we all pushed through. We did it. This would be my first lesson of "not quitting" under tough circumstances. I may not have been good, or even remotely funny, but I pushed my way to the end, did my time, and felt somewhat satisfied.

All I remember from the car ride home was that Jay was driving, it was dark, Sandy was sleeping in the front passenger seat. Dave and I were just confused and laughing. Oh, and that I kept trying to wake Sandy up by doing my one and only "Senor Sexy" voice in his ear. Senor Sexy, as you will learn about later, is an infamous open mic guy from Side Splitters.

After that first trip, and having so much fun, we all began to talk. The 4 of us, compared to the other open mic guys, were a bit older. We shared more life experiences. There were just things we could talk about that most of the other comics couldn't.

Another trip was planned to Nashville, at a well known open mic. I had already planned a road trip for myself to Memphis and Tunica, MS, that same night. I just needed to get away for a bit. I had never, in my life, taken a road trip by myself. This would be the first.

The original plan was that I would spend a night in Memphis going to a concert, then a night in Tunica, MS, and then the 3rd night meet the other 3 guys in Nashville for the open mic. That was the original plan.

Well, Tunica is well known for its casinos. Somehow, on a table game that I had never played before, I won $1,500.00 on the night before the Nashville show. So, obviously, I was overconfident, and called the other guys to cancel. I knew that I had to keep playing on and stay an extra night.

Short story.... I lost all of my money, missed the open mic in Nashville, and missed the conversation on the ride home that they had about creating a group called the "Mid Life Crisis Comics."

What Just Happened?

We are now the Mid Life Crisis Comics. The 4 of us. We would take pictures in the Side Splitters main showroom. Things were moving fast, and I think we were all just engulfed in the situation at hand.

There were a lot of things going on with all of our family lives. We were all overwhelmed. Nobody really knew what was going on. We didn't all have the same goals, and, not too long after it all started, it was down to 3. Dave would end up going in another direction. There was no animosity, it was just one of those "artistic" things I guess. Honestly, I can't remember how it ended up that way, it just did. Next thing I knew, it was just Jay, Sandy, and I.

The four of us. Myself, Sandy, Jay, and Dave.

The Next Phase

It happened so fast. The next thing I know, Jay and Sandy and I were spending a lot of time together. Writing jokes, meeting at each other's houses, at the club. We were creating a group "persona." Everyone started referring to us as the Mid Life Crisis Comics. We traveled frequently to the historic Comedy Catch in Chattanooga, to Nashville. We had confidence in what we were doing.

Being the new guy, I was soaking it all in. Jay, to this day, is the funniest person I've ever been around away from the stage. Period. There is no one else like him. I've met a lot of funny people in my life, tons of amazing comics, both famous and not, yet there is nobody that I have found to light up a room like Jay. I'm not just saying this because he is one of my closest friends. He honestly just "has" it.

Then you have Sandy. My mentor. Nobody, and I mean nobody, has taught me more or made me a better comic than him. Not club owners, other comedians, or anybody else associated with the business. His experience, perspective, and overall knowledge of how to be successful is the reason so many looked up to him. Furthermore, I have been lucky enough to not only be associated with him, but to be one of his closest friends.

I've been a lucky guy.

Jay, Sandy, and myself after a show at the Rocky Top Playhouse in Sevierville, TN

I could easily go into detail here about all of the great shows we did together, but I'm saving those for later. There are, however, several events and shows that are specific to only the M.L.C. Comics, so let me go ahead and tell you about those.

That first year, after gaining some confidence at Side Splitters, the 3 of us began to branch out a little more. There were many trips to Chattanooga and the Comedy Catch, where we would perform at the notorius "Giggles Grill" open mic. Sandy had mentioned it often, and I can clearly remember the first trip. The Comedy Catch was exactly what I had always imagined a comedy club would look and feel like. Old school. Brick walls. Black and white pictures of every famous comedian you have ever heard of on the wall. Signed. Intimidation. Fun. Pressure. It had it all.

We were always welcomed there. We made many great friends, both with comics and fans. What would start as just going and getting on the open mic list would turn into, in a short amount of time, us being asked to headline the open mic. That would eventually lead us to performing in the main showroom, which I had, after the first trip, made a personal goal. Even to this day, I have not performed in a room like that.

With some of our best friends. Grady Ray, Myself, Sandy, Jay, Kristine Kinsey, and Jerry Harvey. One of many amazing nights.

Also, during that first year, we would start our own open mic in Alcoa, TN. Alcoa is in between Knoxville and Sevierville for those wondering. Sandy knew a bar owner there, and he agreed to let us try it out. The Bullpen. A name many comics from a few years ago in the East Tennessee area will remember for a long time to come.

We were there every week for a while. For months. Some nights were packed. One night we performed for 4 people, and that included the bartender and the waitress. There were fights in the crowd, during shows. One of the fights involved other comics. Of course none of us helped him because we were busy arguing over who got to use that as future material.

They played pool during our shows. They yelled at us to shut up. They cussed us out. Jay even got rushed on the stage by a woman because he offended her. When I say stage, I mean a corner of the bar, where the dartboards were.

While this might sound horrific to most, for myself, it was some of the best experiences performing I would ever have. Many nights, not only there, I would be ready to throw in the towel and just bomb based on the crowd and the surroundings. Sandy would always push me though, and made sure I was getting better every single time I grabbed a mic. It was very similar to when you try to tell a child something, they think you are stupid, do it anyway, and thank you later. That was how Sandy was with me. Always pushing me, even though I didn't think it was relevant at the time. Jay, on the other hand, we didn't worry about. He was always laid back, confident. Even when he bombed, he would walk off the stage and say "Boys. I killed it." Always made me smile.

Not only were we spending a lot of time doing shows, writing, and talking about comedy, we were becoming close friends. We were all from different backgrounds, walks of life. However, we were all 3 good guys. We were family oriented. All of us had children, and our worlds revolved around our families. That was part of the reason we were the Mid Life Crisis Comics. The other part was that we were all 3 getting older and fairly nuts in our own special way.

During this first year we were becoming staples at Side Splitters. We practically lived there. We were there for every open mic. We were there on weekends hanging out with the national headliner and other comics. Sometimes, one of us was performing on the weekends in the main showroom, so the other 2 of us would always be there for support.

One night, while sitting around throwing out ideas, we made a decision to try something out of the box. We decided to go on a tour, to L.A., to perform at the world famous Comedy Store. We had officially lost our minds at this point.

Not only would we do a 2 week tour from Knoxville to L.A., we would do our kickoff show at Side Splitters, in the main showroom, on a Sunday night. On top of that, as if we couldn't get any bolder, we would have 100 t-shirts made for the event. Things were lining up to be a disaster. Or would it?

The M.L.C. Kickoff Show #1

We honestly didn't know what to expect. The show was scheduled for Sunday, March 13, 2011 at Side Splitters. We would do the show, hop in the car afterwards, and start making our way to L.A. We were hoping for a big crowd for the kickoff show, both because the bigger the show the more fun, and we needed money for the trip.

The weeks leading up to the show were spent promoting. I can't remember promoting any show more than we did for that night. We knew it had to be huge for many reasons. We had shirts made specifically for the tour, hoping to make some extra cash for the long 2 week trip. I got the KIA ready for the 7,000 roundtrip miles we were about to embark upon. I was nervous on every level.

The show was to be a normal hour and half show, typical for comedy clubs. Coley, another comic and one of the managers at Side Splitters would be our host. Jay would kick things off, then myself, with Sandy to close it out. We would each do 20 to 30 minutes. This was going to be my longest performance to date, and hopefully in front of a packed crowd.

Fellow Comedian Kristine Kinsey's goat, sporting our Mid Life Crisis T-shirt. As far as I know, it's the only goat that bought one.

The night of the show, as usual, I showed up very early. My bags were packed. The anticipation had been driving me crazy for weeks. I was ready to go, excited, but also a little uncertain since I had never been away from my kids for that long. That was really the only part I wasn't looking forward to.

I spent at least an hour pacing outside, memorizing my set, on the side of the building. This would be my normal spot for a few years. For this show, like I mentioned before, I would be performing my longest set so far, roughly 25 minutes. Remember, I had only been doing stand-up comedy for 13 months at this point.

About an hour before the show, I started to notice cars pouring into the parking lot. I was in shock. I already knew we had sold quite a few tickets online, but I had assumed that many of those were just friends being nice and trying to support us, with no intention of coming to a show on a Sunday night. I was wrong.

At around 7:30, roughly half an hour before show time, the lobby was packed. The little tiny room that I had stumbled in just 13 months prior for my first open mic, was now packed with friends, family, and fans to see the 3 of us. They were buying shirts before the show, and we were signing them! My first autographs. It was a surreal feeling, and one that I will never forget.

Friends and fans, Tammy and Angie, wearing their Mid Life Crisis Comics shirts to the show. Myself in shock, Jay cool as usual.

The show itself was incredible. Almost a sold out crowd, over 200 people. The main showroom was electric. It was an experience I had only had one time in my life before, and that was my high school senior year playing basketball in front of thousands of people.

Coley did an amazing job getting the crowd ready. Jay, was Jay. He killed it, not only in his own mind, but really killed it. My set went better than I ever could have dreamed of. Then, Sandy finished the show strong, like he always did.

To top it off, the 4 of us got on stage together at the end for a little fun. We told stories, did some impromptu games, and put on a show. I hate to use the word "magical", but that's exactly what it was.

Don't ask.

The show was a success. Nearly sold out a major comedy club on a Sunday night. Sold close to 100 t-shirts. We were funny. Signed autographs. Made money. We were surrounded by friends and family. This night, there wasn't really anything else I could ask for. It was about as perfect as it gets.

After the show, we spent time hanging out with everyone in the lounge. The same tiny lounge that I had performed at just 13 months ago for the first time. Yeah, I know I keep saying that. But it's important.

Several goodbyes later, we were in the KIA. We were on our way to L.A. This would be the trip of a lifetime.

The First Mid Life Crisis Comics Tour

The emotions were running high. We had just completed the first night of the tour, and it was so much more than we could have even imagined.

It took about 3 minutes in the car for us all to finally exhale. What a high. Each of us knew we had killed it that night, made a ton of money (in comedy terms, and especially since I was only 13 months in.) We had over 200 people show up on a Sunday night in March to see us perform. My first fear had been conquered. Now, it was time to take it to another level. It's time to see how we can do in states outside of the Southeast.

Our first stop would be Dallas, TX, where my mother, Anna, lives. She had never seen me perform, so we made it a priority to go there. It would be nearly impossible to make up the scenario that would happen in Dallas. It was really that weird.

My Weirdest Show Ever?

Not only does my mother live in the Dallas area, but so does my brother Dax and his family. Neither of them had ever seen me perform, so I was both excited and nervous. This tour was planned, and it was a combination of bars and comedy clubs. This one would be a bar in downtown Dallas, and it was unlike anything I had ever experienced comedy wise.

To make things interesting, it was also my mother's 60th birthday celebration. She invited several of her friends to come check out the show and party with her. Prior to the show, however, her and her friends, myself, my brother, Jay, and Sandy would go out for dinner to celebrate her birthday. I would learn a very hard lesson this night pertaining to my future stand up performances.

My mom and I have always been big wine drinkers, so naturally, at dinner, we ordered a couple of bottles for the group. Up to this point in my short time doing stand up, I had not had any wine before a show.

We went to a Mediterranean restaurant close to the venue, drank our wine and ate some incredible food, then parted ways. Jay and Sandy and myself always liked to get there early, meet the other comics, and hangout. I would see my mother, brother, and her friends later at the show. Before they would arrive, however, it would already start getting weird.

We literally drive across the street, park, and walk into this huge bar. It's split down the middle. On the right, mainly just a bar with tables. On the left, a stage with more tables. In the back, there is an outdoor patio wedged into an alley. It's a pretty cool place.

Just as I expected, I slur. I can't remember my jokes. I'm staring at my mom, who is smiling at me with that proud look on her face. I'm internally angry, because I know that I was bombing. I had grown accustomed to "not" bombing, especially the night before at Side Splitters where I had just given my best performance to date. My frustration took over me, making things worse. The words just wouldn't come out of my mouth. In the crowd I see Jay, Sandy, my brother, my mom and her friends, the Superhero, the Washboard guy, and all the other interesting characters scattered among the onlookers. I totally blew it.

The Dyer Street Bar, Dallas, TX. The place I would officially get humbled, and embarrass myself in front of my mother.

After the show, we hop in the car, and make the drive back to my mother's house. It's about 45 minutes outside of the city. I was distraught. The entire ride home, I keep saying "But I'm funny! I promise! It was the wine! And the superhero and the washboard guy! Seriously mom, I promise I can do this!"

We get back to her house. Her friends are there. Jay and Sandy are there. We are all sitting there watching TV. I'm frustrated. I had worked so hard, in just over a year, to get better every time I got on stage. I had accomplished more than many comics had in 5 years already. Yet, this night, I totally blew it. In front of my mom. I just went to bed.

The next morning, though, I woke up to find my mother and Sandy sitting in front of a laptop. She was dying laughing. Almost tears in her eyes. I stumble over slowly, still reeling from the wine the night before, only to see them watching my performance from Side Splitters 2 nights before. She said "Wow! You really are good at this honey!"

Sandy saved me. This is the special bond that Sandy, Jay and I will always have. We always...always have each other's backs. Always.

Back On The Road

After a couple of days at my mother's house, hitting theme parks and hanging out, we jump back in the KIA for our quest to L.A. My mom has literally packed a huge box full of food. I think we ate the entire thing before we got to Waco, which was not that far away.

In order to keep this book less than a thousand pages, or at least this chapter anyway, I'm going to skip ahead. Our next stop would be Oklahoma City, then Las Vegas. In between, some weirdness in New Mexico. I could literally write an entire chapter on this short stretch, but the book would go in a direction not appropriate for everyone, it would be too long, and, in all honesty, it would have very little to do with comedy. Instead, though, I will just put a couple pictures of myself along the way. How's that?

You really didn't think I would leave this pic of me standing on the side of the road in New Mexico, with a cowboy hat on that I bought at a gas station in Texas, and that was getting me honked at by truckers, out of the book did you?

I bet you really didn't think I'd do back to back pictures did you?
Well, here you go. Me, in Las Vegas, wearing ginormous sunglasses.
Apparently, I actually had paid for them and owned them at the time
of this picture.

We Made It

Finally, we make it to Los Angeles. 2,200 miles later, and we are there. Our goal is in sight. The world famous Comedy Store. We don't even know if we are going to get a spot. Will one of us get on? Two of us? All 3 of us? Who knows. We just need a hotel room at this point. We will worry about getting on the show later that evening.

So, this is going to sound a little crazy to those who aren't comedians. We drove 2,200 miles to "hopefully" get 3 minutes on stage at an open mic. That's it. There was no plan. We didn't know how it worked. We didn't know how to sign up. We literally knew nothing. We got in the car in Knoxville, after a sold out show, and drove for days for something that was unrealistic. We were having so much fun, to be honest, that we didn't really care. But, actually, we did care.

After checking in to our hotel room, that we had originally thought was closer to the Comedy Store than it was, we chilled out. It was a last minute hotel choice, based off of our 2011 phone map. Might as well have been a map from 1912. Anyway, we were just happy to be there. The hotel was older but swanky at the same time. Compared to what we had experienced before, except for Las Vegas, it was pretty sweet. We were rolling L.A. style.

As usual, we decide to go to the show pretty early. When you are doing open mics, you really don't know what to expect. Normally, it's better to get there before everyone else. Sometimes, however, it doesn't really matter, as we would find out this particular night.

I made the mistake of convincing Jay and Sandy that we should just walk to the Comedy Store from our hotel. It was only a few blocks. I had no idea that a monsoon would hit us on the way.

We were videotaping the entire trip. It would be months later, after watching the video, that I finally saw the look on their faces, as we were walking up a steep hill to the show, getting pelted by rain. At the time, though, I remember laughing as I walked backwards up that hill, saying "Isn't this fun? What an adventure!?"

Finally, we make it to the Comedy Store. Soaked. We didn't care though. We had made it. I was so nervous, I was honestly hoping that I didn't get a spot. I had been doing stand up for only 13 months, and here I am standing outside of one of the pinnacles of stand up comedy. This is where many of the biggest names had started. I didn't belong there. But....but....I came so far. Please give me a spot. No, don't. I'll just watch. No, really...I'll take a spot. I don't know. Whatever is fine. Just...just don't give me a spot. If you do give me a spot, please don't be first. Just don't give me one. That will be easier. Or, maybe just give me one and I'll be ok.

This was my brain at the time.

We had no idea of how the process worked. We show up early. It's still pouring rain. We are drenching wet. There are a few people there. We sign up. We still don't know how it works. We are standing outside, under a covered bar/porch area. More people start coming. Before we know it, there are 50 comics standing underneath this small area. We try to mask our confusion, excitement, and eagerness by mingling with the L.A. people. I'm a wreck. Bad.

After talking to the regulars, we find out that only 15 comics make the list, and they won't post it until 5 minutes before the 7pm show time. Great, just great. The odds of all 3 of us, or any of us making the list, is slim to none. We drove over 2,000 miles for nothing. Or did we?

We start making phone calls and texts back to Side Splitters. I don't know why we did that. They were in Tennessee, we were in California. What could they do? Make a phone call? It was worth a shot though. That was our reasoning. We had come too far.

After a lot of confusion, and rain, the guy comes out and posts the list, 5 minutes before the show would start. It's like a pack of wolves to see who made it. All of the regulars assumed they made it, and were just looking to see *which* spot they got. Jay, Sandy, and myself were the last ones to see the list. We got stuck in the back of the pack, trying to peek over shoulders to no avail. As the crowd cleared, we finally go to see.

We were all 3 on the list. What????

Ok, so now I'm nervous. I'm on the list. We had spent over an hour mingling with the regulars, listening to their stories of how difficult it was to get on the list, how important it was, and of all the famous comedians who had started in this exact same position. Great, just great.

We get to go in. The Comedy Store is divided into different showrooms, as are many comedy clubs. We were to be on the most basic one. We had 3 minutes. That's it. In Knoxville, those 3 minutes would be equal to 20 minutes and a feature spot.

The show starts, and the first comic goes up. It took about 10 seconds for me to feel better. Thousands of miles and days of worrying, and it was ok. This would be another lesson. Comics are comics. Funny people are funny. Some comics aren't funny. Some are. Where you are from has no bearing. You are either good, or you aren't. Period.

The 3 of us were scattered among the list. Sandy did well, even with a microphone malfunction. Jay did well. I did well, even though, as usual, I got mad at my joke selection. I always do that, however, so it wasn't a big deal.

The show ends. I think we are done for the night. Next thing I know, we are being escorted to the next showroom to watch. Apparently our phone calls and texts to Side Splitters back home worked. They were treating us well.

We got to go backstage, meeting the comics for the upcoming show in the main room. These comics were headliners at major comedy clubs we knew, personalities from television shows we had seen. The Comedy Store is so big, so famous, that these comics were only getting 10 minutes. This was a big deal for us back home. In Knoxville, getting to do 10 minutes meant you were doing so well you were close to featuring. In L.A., comics who were used to being the main attraction and doing 45 minutes to an hour in other parts of the country were lucky to get 10 minutes. It was a different world. I was paying attention, learning.

During the night, we kept hearing rumors that limos were pulling up in the parking lot with some of the most famous comedians in the world. At first I was excited to see some of these television personalities, but that dream would soon be crushed, as we would learn that they had their own "special" showroom where they practiced new material. It was still an incredible feeling to know that I was sharing the same building with them, even if I had just performed for 3 minutes.

After a while, exhaustion hit all of us. It had been a long trip to get here, and the stress and anxiety of getting a spot on the show had overwhelmed us. So, we decided to walk back to the hotel room and crash. No L.A. partying this time. We had a long trip to Houston, TX the next day.

The Rest Of The Tour

Before you hear it from Jay and Sandy, I'm just going to say it here. Yes, we drove my KIA on this trip. Yes, Jay and Sandy drove a majority of the time. Yes, I was supposed to drive a long stretch from L.A. to Houston. Yes, I got tired and quit after 2 hours. There. It's over.

The rest of the trip found us hitting Houston, Baton Rouge and New Orleans, before heading home. Houston, as it happened often, would be Jay and Sandy sleeping in hotel room during the day while I was shopping at the mall. This was just our trend. I was restless, always, unless I had to drive.

New Orleans was, to say the least, interesting. I'm just going to summarize this here in one paragraph. First, Jay books us in a hotel room near Bourbon St. Its features consisted of a crazy cat at the front desk and extremely slanted floors in the bedrooms. Next, we sampled some of the famous "Hurricanes", because, well, I think it's a law there that you have to? I don't know. Next thing I know, a man shining my shoes takes all of the money out of wallet. Every dollar. Then, Jay talks to a horse, asking him "why the long face?", which happened to be occupied by a police officer, who abruptly told us to move along. After that, I apparently was singing karaoke in front of a large crowd (we know this because of video.) The night ended with us walking back to the hotel, videotaping and interviewing people, with Jay continuously getting threatened of being slapped.

That was our first tour. It was 2 weeks of interesting shows, interesting people. We rode rollercoasters, visited the world's largest meteor crater, spent time with my mother and brother. We did a lot. Most importantly, we created a special bond that will never be broken. Jay and Sandy are like brothers to me.

This is how slanted the floors were in the hotel room in New Orleans. I'm obviously sliding right off the bed.

Hitting Bourbon Street early. You know, before the horses and people who took all my money came.

The Second Tour

About a year after the first tour, we decided to do it again. This one would be shorter though. We were strapped for time, so we decided to cut this one to a week and go up north to New York City.

Once again, we had another Sunday night kickoff show at Side Splitters. This one didn't sell out like the first one, but it was still a big crowd. We jumped in the car and headed for Baltimore, which, as it turned out, would be the best show of the trip.

At this point in my short comedy span, I was gaining confidence. As you will read later, I was headlining my own show in Sevierville, a house emcee at Side Splitters, and featuring for some special events. Baltimore would be another test.

As far as open mics and showcases went, this room was packed with some serious talent. There were headlining Underground comics and guys who had been on TV. The place was big, and it was packed. My friends, Kim and Kent, who I hadn't seen in forever, were there. I was once again feeling some pressure to do well. I got bumped a spot for an unexpected headliner who wanted to do some time. That put even more pressure on me. Unlike most open mics, they gave us 15 minutes each since we were touring from out of town.

As usual, Jay and Sandy were there to help me. Sandy was always teaching, always telling me what I did right and did wrong. Jay was the motivator. He always just gave you that look and said "Kill it."

I ended up having one of my best sets to date, especially in a bar setting. Jay and Sandy did well as usual. This was a great start to our week long northeast spree.

The rest of the week is kind of a blur. That first show in Baltimore was so good, all I can remember from the rest of the trip was having fun. We hit Jersey Shore, rode some rollercoasters again, hit New York City for a couple days. The other shows were really uneventful. It was almost as if we were taking a break from comedy, while being on a comedy tour. Back home, we were doing so many shows, all over the place, that it was exhausting. This was like a vacation where we got to periodically tell some jokes without pressure, and just enjoy the rest.

Jay got lost while we were on a tour of Good Morning America. When Sandy and I found him, he was on the set hanging out with the crew while the show was going on. Typical Jay, smooth talking his way in. We would get to hang out there for the rest of the show.

This trip would be the last tour we did together. Not by choice. I'm sure we would all do it 10 times a year if possible. Family life, work, and our own separate directions of comedy would finally sink in. Now, we still take trips together, but not comedy related. We take the families, eat good food, and ride rollercoasters. We hang out at each other's house. Every so often, if we are lucky, we do a show together. Maybe again, one day, we can go on another one of these magical tours.

Jersey Shore. Unfortunately, Jay couldn't find anyone there to sweet talk to get us on the show.

My New Life

In the first few days of February, 2012, I met a couple friends at Side Splitters before a show. Over dinner, they told me about their friend in Georgia who was also recently divorced with children. They thought she and I would be good match to go out. So, I started texting her. We texted all that night. I was literally texting her before I went up on stage. About what? Couldn't tell you.

Just a little recap for you. I was separated in early 2010. I was officially divorced in early 2011. I had 50% custody of my boys. In October of 2011, after running out of money from leaving my banking career to pursue comedy full time, I moved to Seymour, TN, and into my Grandparents' old house, rent free. This was supposed to be short term, until I figured out what I was actually doing.

Friday, February 10, 2012, I was hosting my own show in Sevierville. My good friends Coor Cohen and Riley Fox were the feature and headliner that night. Jenny texts me that she wants me to officially come to Chattanooga to meet her in person! So, I tell Coor and Riley that I will have to leave as soon as I do the upfront hosting duties. They understand and I hit the road.

At that time, I was exactly 2 years into pursuing comedy. Besides my kids, stand-up comedy was my life. I was living in Seymour, about 45 minutes from Side Splitters. My kids both went to school 45 minutes away. When I had the boys, I was driving. I was spending time with them. I coached their basketball games. When they weren't with me, I was performing. Somewhere. That was it.

I make the 2 hour drive to Chattanooga from Sevierville to meet her. I'm anxious. I'm telling myself "don't like her too much. You have to focus on comedy and the boys. Matter of fact, let's just not like her at all. Yeah, she seems cool by text and phone, but I just don't need this at all right now. I've got too much going on and my life is already hectic." I never contemplated turning around, however, I seriously considered just staying for 5 minutes and leaving. As I get closer to Chattanooga, I pull over and put the address in the KIA's GPS for the bar her and her friends were at. It was getting real now.

The first couple of months were crazy. We would spend every second together as possible. We didn't want to meet each other's kids, not just yet. Although, in the back of our minds, that was coming. We both knew this was meant to be. We just had to be careful. We had both been through so much. However, we also knew that we didn't want to waste time.

As you read earlier, I went on a quick tour with Jay and Sandy to New York City. This wasn't long after I had met Jenny. I literally spent the entire trip texting her from the backseat, driving the both of them nuts. I don't think the 2 of them will ever let me live that down.

It wasn't long after I got back from that quick tour before we decided to meet each other's kids. Jenny was still living in Georgia, a few hours away, so it wasn't easy. We were so careful not to disrupt their everyday lives. Getting married was inevitable. How we were going to go about it? That was the hard question.

Jenny, Ethan, and Jacob. Once again, I'm a lucky guy.

In late May of 2012, roughly only 4 months after we met, Jenny and the boys moved to Seymour to live with us. According to many of our friends and family, we were moving too fast. However, we knew. We just knew. Why waste time? Life is too short, and we were happy together. The kids were out of school for the summer. It was the perfect time.

Luckily, they all hit off it pretty quickly. Yes, the boys are all unique. They have their differences. But it was much easier than expected. We eventually got to where we could sync the kids schedules, to where we would either have all of them, most of them, or none of them. We were so crazy, driving back and forth to Georgia, or Knoxville, or basketball games, or soccer games. When the kids were gone, I was doing shows. It was chaos at its finest.

In July of 2012, while in the Cleveland, OH area for her grandfather's funeral, I proposed. We both knew I was going to do it soon, but we didn't know exactly when. I proposed at a place I knew was special to both her and her family, although I know the timing sounds weird. It wasn't though. It made sense.

Jenny's entire family is amazing. Her parents, her grandparents, uncles, cousins, nephews, nieces. All of them. Incredible people. While at the funeral, for a wonderful man that I unfortunately never had the pleasure to meet, I had the feeling it was time. I know it sounds weird, but it just felt right. I still was unsure of exactly how to do it. I already had the blessing of her parents. I was just nervous of how to go about it, and when to do it.

After the funeral, we all went to her grandparent's house. I heard some of the most inspiring stories about her papa. Jenny's entire family was there. They brought food, and just spent time telling heartfelt stories about this man who meant so much to all of them.

At some point, Jenny took me to the backyard, where her papa had his garden. It was simple, yet elegant. I was conflicted. I wanted to ask her to marry me, but I wasn't sure if this was the right time. I honestly didn't know what to do.

It seemed like a lifetime. I was listening to her father tell me stories of himself and his siblings as kids, doing something off the roof of the garage, right near the garden. I can literally picture it. I just can't remember the exact words. It was something about making army men or airplanes or something and jumping off the roof. I know that's probably not right, but it's all I remember. I was so nervous, knowing what I was about to do. My mind was in so many places at the same time. What would I do?

Let's just say, I did it, and she said yes. I don't think there is a need for more words here. The picture is enough.

Now that we were engaged, we decided to not waste time. She had been married and divorced. I had been married and divorced, twice. Together we made the decision to just have a small wedding and make it a party, and to do it soon.

November 3, 2012, 9 months after we met, we got married. It was a unique wedding to say the least. Many of our friends and family were there. We were happy. Just being us. Right after the actual ceremony, performed by her father, we rolled out a huge television to watch the Tennessee football game. There is a picture of myself wearing a suit and Jenny in her dress, lying on the floor in front of the TV, with the kids around us. Yeah, I know. I know. It happened though, and we enjoyed it. Afterwards, Jenny and I retired to our hotel room, where we had cigars and wine, laughed and just enjoyed being together. It was us, and it always will be.

Our happy, crazy family, on our wedding day in 2012.

Since our wedding day, the last 3 years have been filled with a lot of love, tons of driving, basketball games, basketball practices, concerts, school functions, homework, Jenny going back to school, both of us working full time, more driving, fun weekend getaways (rare, but amazing when they happen), me doing shows and writing books, friends, and chaos. It's been the best 3 years of my life. Hands down.

Since this book is mostly about comedy, let me tell you about our "comedy home life." You see, most of my friends who are comedians are either very young without kids or not married, or older and whose kids are already grown. There are a few exceptions, yes, but for the most part, this is the way it is.

I must admit, I am very lucky. I have a partner, a wife, who is not only supportive of my odd career choice, but who actually comes to almost every show! Many of our fondest experiences together have been related to doing some weird event together. Comedy clubs, bars, charity events, festivals, corporate shows, and just some plain weird places. We've done it all, together. I've almost quit a couple of times, but she believes in me, and pushes me through. Like I said, I'm a lucky man.

Jenny and I before my first show ever at the infamous Zanie's Comedy Club in Nashville. Her beautiful smile always calms my nerves. Every time.

I don't know if the kids think I'm funny or not. I think my oldest son, Weston, does. He's a comedy junkie, so I really don't know. He's the only one who has actually seen me do my normal thing. The other 3 have been to a few of my G rated shows, and I think they laughed. Who knows. All I know is that I hope they are proud of me, regardless of whether or not they think I'm funny.

Really. It's a weird life. It's a weird profession. Constantly wondering if your kids look up to you or not. Honestly, sometimes, I don't know if I want them to, especially when I get home from performing in front of 3 people in a bar for $13. However, it's what I do. One day, I hope, they will see the sacrifices I've made, the late nights, the horrible money, and say "Yeah...Dad did what he loved, and made sure we had what we needed, and it all paid off."

If not, then that means I'll be working a regular job sometime soon, after this book is released.

Either way, I'm a lucky guy. I can honestly say I have the best family in the world.

Love.

Doing It My Way

I know this chapter will attract some critics from the comedy world. From club owners, touring comedians, and anybody associated in the world of comedy. It's not a long chapter, but it's something that I need to say.

In 5 short years, I've accomplished more than many. I've performed in front of 1,000 people. I've made enough money from comedy alone to file a tax return in 4 of them. I've written a book, sold thousands of copies, with 100% good reviews (unless you include my kids, they just don't get it.)

But where am I going? What is my place? Am I a club comic? Am I a touring club comic? Am I an Underground comic? Am I a corporate entertainer? Am I just a hometown, bar hopping comic? What am I?

Let me tell you what I am.

I'm a Husband. I'm a Father. I'm a comic. Period. I can perform an hour PG, or R, or whatever needed in front of any crowd. I don't mean to sound over confident. I've just worked hard at what I do. I realized early on that I needed to be different. When you have kids, and you choose to pursue a profession that demands a lot of work that is unconventional, away from your family, you tend to try to perfect it quickly.

Now, I'm not saying I'm perfect. I'm far from it. If I knew exactly what I was doing, I would have been on TV by now. I've been close, but too many other factors have gotten in the way. Yes, I work hard at what I do, but my family comes first, so I'm constantly finding ways to avoid going all the way. Am I afraid of taking the next step, worrying what it would do to my normal family life? Possibly, yes. Ok, yes. I am.

When I started this crazy ride, it was in a comedy club. Side Splitters in Knoxville. That's where I started learning. Eventually, with the help of Sandy and Jay, I started branching out to bars and other venues. I've pretty much done any weird show you could imagine. Trust me.

My first comedy promo picture. Please, don't laugh too hard.

I have a lot of options. I could really hit the comedy club scene hard, featuring 3 to 5 nights a week in cities all over the country. I could tour constantly as a Headlining Underground comic, hitting bars, small theaters, and odd and end venues all over the place. I could put myself in a place to be a corporate comedian, primarily doing company Christmas parties, events, etc., and making great money. I could do any of these things. I've done all of them at one point or another.

The fact is, I enjoy all of them. I could easily see myself doing any of the above. Most of the successful comedians you have seen on TV have taken the comedy club route. There are some that have taken the Underground option and made it big. The corporate comics, well, that is another thing. They are often unseen but very successful in their own right, especially monetarily.

At one point or another, I've gone through phases where I started to pinpoint my direction. I started out as a comedy club guy. Period. That's exactly where I pictured my future. I was terrible in a bar setting, but I excelled in the clubs. I had a fan base. I was comfortable. I emceed, featured, and kind of headlined (as part of a group of headliners.) I was certain this was my direction.

Then, many things in my life changed. I started my own bar show, I got remarried and doubled my family. Or quadrupled it, depending on your math preference. The Knoxville comedy scene was changing, on a daily basis. Everything was different.

Next thing I knew, I started getting requests for charity and family oriented events. I began focusing on cleaner material. It started with 10 minutes. Then was 20. Then 35. Then an hour. Before long, I was being offered $500 to do 20 minutes. That changed everything. To make that same money in a club or bar, doing R rated material, I would have to work 5 nights to equal one night of PG corporate show.

3 years into comedy, I wrote my first book. In the beginning, it was just something to sell at shows instead of t-shirts or bumper stickers. I had no idea the success that it would bring. Not monetarily, but exposure. It sent me in a new direction that I didn't see coming.

Here is my point in all of this. I enjoy being on a stage. I love to make people laugh. That's it. Really, that's it. Am I the best at it? No. Am I good at it? Yes. Do I work hard at it? Yes. Just being honest.

Unlike many comedians out there, I can't honestly say that I've spent my whole life leading up to this. It really just fell in my lap. I've always been goofy, probably over the top goofy while trying to be funny at times. I've had many people say "Yeah...you were always funny." There's a difference from just being funny and being a stand-up comedian, though. Being funny is easy. The "doing it on stage thing" is not.

However, when you are 36 years old, and a single Dad with 2 kids, you have to make a decision when dealing with a newfound hobby. You either go all out, focus, and make yourself stand out. Or, you just try it and move on quickly. There really isn't a grey area here. You don't have time or money to waste. It's either "do this!" or "yeah, that was a cool experience."

Yes, maybe I was a bit selfish in the beginning. I was in a rough place mentally, and I needed an out. I was enjoying myself. I also knew, though, that I had what it took to make it. I had a maturity and drive that most of the other comics didn't have yet. I spent many nights lying in bed, trying to figure out what to do.

Not long after I had made the decision to go for it 100%, leave my job as a banker, move out of my condo, I met Jenny. That's when my focus would change again.

At first, after she and I met, it was still carefree. It was "yeah, I'll do that show for free." Or "Yeah, I'll be there. Hopefully we will get some tips." Once we got married, though, things changed. I had to get picky, for 2 reasons.

First of all, my family went from myself and 2 boys, to myself, Jenny, and 4 boys. The money was tight. I couldn't just do my normal 3 or 4 nights a week of shows, when the kids were gone, making little to nothing. It just wasn't practical.

Second, I just enjoyed spending time with Jenny and the boys. Period. Whether we were traveling, or doing stuff around town, or just sitting home watching movies. I wanted to be with them.

This...this is my wonderful family. This is why I do things my way.

So, here I am. What do I do? Do I just hit the road and do shows 3 or 4 nights a week, either in clubs or bars, and leave my family? Do I just stay home, and wait for the corporate shows to roll in, doing local bar shows here and there for $100 every once in a while?

That's the question. It's a question that I can't answer yet. As of now, I'm just doing my own thing. I'm picking and choosing which shows I do. If it fits my schedule, around my family, then maybe. I have basketball games to go to, kids' music concerts to attend. I have important life events that only happen once to make sure I'm there.

If the money, time, and travel is worth it, and I don't have to miss something important with either Jenny or the kids, then maybe. It's on my own terms. I'm doing it my way.

Criticize me all you want. Tell me "I'm not doing what it takes to be successful." Tell me "You'll never make it doing it that way." Don't' book me because I don't fit your schedule. I don't care. Life is too short to worry about what everyone else tells you is important.

I love my wife. I love my kids. I love comedy. You want to book me, then get on the list. I've already proven that I can be successful in other professions. Yes, I would absolutely love to make it doing stand-up comedy full time. Of course I would. However, I'm not going to jeopardize the short amount of time I get to spend with my family just because it's "what I'm supposed to do."

There is a reason many comedians, both famous and not, are so miserable. It's not only comedians, either. Every profession. Too many people try so hard to be successful, only to give up the things that mean the most. I'm not doing it. Ever.

If you ever see me on Comedy Central, or on any other television network, just remember this. I worked hard to get there. I didn't sacrifice what was important to me. I didn't leave my family 4 days a week to pursue a dream.

If you see me there, one day, remember.... I did what it took to make it, on my own terms, without worrying that my family missed me most of the time. I was there, for all of their events. Front row.

If I am doing a show, you know what is important to me? It's seeing Jenny in the crowd, smiling, laughing. It's knowing that I can be myself on stage without wishing that I was at one of the kid's events that I should be at. Yeah, sure, every once in a while the boys will stay with my dad while Jenny and I do a show a few minutes away. It's not often though, and we never miss anything important. Ever.

Am I saying that I'm better than other comics who have families? Of course not. It's just a personal choice. Some of my best friends' tour, make good money, and provide for their family doing comedy. I respect that, 100%. It's just not for me, not yet anyway. One day, I envision Jenny and I hitting the road, traveling, seeing the world, and making people laugh along the way. It will happen. I'm sure about that.

Every Night Is An Experience

It's time to shift focus now. You've read about what lead me here. You, by now, know what my purpose is. You know my background, my family life, my early years.

The next several chapters are going to focus on specific shows I've done. The incredible nights and events that I absolutely love, even when they were weird and not so pleasant. To simplify things, I'm going to break the rest of this up into sections by show type.

Before I begin, though, let me give you a brief rundown on the different kinds of shows that I do. It will help you better understand exactly what comedians, and myself, go through on a nightly basis.

The Bar Shows

Once again, this could be another book by itself. Bar shows are probably the most fascinating of all shows. As a comedian, you NEVER know what you are getting yourself into at a bar. They can be the absolute best of shows, or by far the worst. It's a total crapshoot.

I have probably spent more nights in bars slinging jokes than any other venue over the last 5 years. I love them. I hate them. I'm addicted to them, to be completely honest.

There are several variations of bar shows, too. There are the open mics. 10, 15, 20 comics going up to a rowdy bar to try new material. Usually, 6 to 10 minutes each. I've learned over the years, never go first. Don't go last. If you go first, the audience is still getting settled, still talking, still greeting each other. They aren't listening, at all. If you go last, half of the crowd is drunk, half of the crowd has left. You can't win with either of these scenarios. If you get a choice, go early middle. The crowd has settled, still sober, and still there.

Myself, at the Upstairs Underground Show at Preservation Pub,
February 2011. Knoxville's longest standing Open Mic created by
Matt Ward. This was one of their first shows, and where I would
perform on the night of my 5th anniversary.

There are also traditional shows at bars. When I say traditional, I mean comedy club style. Headliner, Feature, Emcee, and maybe a guest spot. As with the open mic type of shows, these can be interesting. This could turn out to be the worst night ever as a headliner. Everyone could be drunk or gone by the time you get to the mic. It really depends on both the crowd and the comics before you. If they bomb, and the crowd is terrible, you may be talking to 3 drunk people in the end. If the openers do well, and the mood is right, you could have the most fun ever on a stage. Speaking for myself as a headliner, these are my favorite nights. They are exciting and extremely unpredictable.

There are other variations to bar shows. You could be a traveling headliner, coming into an unfamiliar city and performing at an open mic. There could be 20 open mic comics doing 5 to 8 minutes each, with you headlining at the end, doing 30 minutes to an hour. In my experience, these are by far the hardest shows. Your success will depend on how many open mic comics there are, and how well they do. If there are 20 comics doing 6 minutes each, and there are a lot of newcomers, who do poorly (we all have, not knocking them), then it's going to be very difficult for the headliner. The crowd is probably sick of comedy at this point. You better be famous, or just amazing that night. If not, you will end up cussing all the way back to the hotel. I've done that many times.

All in all, bar shows are exciting. They are different. They are unpredictable. The heckling is horrible, yet invigorating. The talking amongst the crowd is overwhelming, yet opens opportunities. There are people there who didn't know a show was happening, get mad, and want to fight you because of what you said on stage. There are people there to drink, to talk to friends, to see the band afterwards. They don't want to hear you. They didn't come for you. Period.

However, if you are funny, and can get their attention, and make them laugh...then...you have just had a night like no other. You were successful, and you leave smiling.

I love bar shows, and always will. No matter what.

Comedy Clubs

The traditional comedy club. This is what everyone thinks of as "Stand Up Comedy." They are probably right, however there are so many other ways to go about it. There's no doubt, though, that this is where most comics want to be. There is good reason for this.

This is where I started. In Knoxville, in 2010, Side Splitters Comedy Club was the place to be. The open mics every Wednesday. The famous, well known headliners Thursday through Saturday. Up and coming, semi famous "feature" comics opening up for the headliners on the weekends. The best of the best locals getting to emcee the shows. It was a magical place. In most mid to big cities still to this day, it's the place to be.

Here is the basic structure of a comedy club. Shows will run, typically, Thursday through Saturday. Some are Wednesday through Sunday. It varies. To simplify things, I'm going to use the Thursday through Saturday structure that Side Splitters used, based on my own experience.

There will be an emcee, many times a local or regional comic who has worked their way up through the open mics at that particular club. They will do 6 to 8 minutes to begin the show. Sometimes they are required to be clean, as it was at Side Splitters, and sometimes not. The emcee will do some material, announcements and general rules of the evening (no heckling, tip your wait staff, etc.) and warm up the crowd. It's a tough job, that' for sure.

Sometimes, randomly, there will be a guest spot. These are also usually regional comics who have done well in the open mics, and are getting an "unpaid" opportunity to perform on the main stage. Most of the time, it's an 8 to 10 minute spot.

Then, there is the feature. The feature, or "middle", is the official opener for the headliner. This position can vary from someone well known from anywhere in the country, to someone the headliner themselves are touring with, to a local who is really doing well. It can change every weekend, depending on who the headliner is.

Last, but not least, you have the headliner. This is who everyone is there to see. They sell the tickets. They are on the posters. They are on the radio before the show. The headliner can be someone currently relevant, like a Last Comic Standing winner or finalist, or a well known name who has been around a while, such as comedians from movies and television in the 70's, 80's, and 90's. Typically, they will do 45 minutes to an hour to close the show, selling merchandise in the lobby afterwards.

Myself and one of my all -time favorite headliners, Carl LaBove. I was not only fortunate enough to perform with him, but to also get personal advice from one of the best (oh, and give him my book!)

Contests

Contests. A word many comics that I know hate to hear. Including myself most of the time. Yet, we do them. Why? Good question.

Plain and simple, contests are weird. In sports, there are clear cut winners in a tournament setting. In comedy, it's subjective, and varies from contest to contest based on both who the judges are and what the criteria is.

When you are just starting out, contests are great. You don't have any expectations, and if you win, you are on top of the world. This happened to me 6 months in, twice, back to back. I thought I was a veteran of the business at that point (I would soon learn I wasn't, however.) But, after a while, once you have begun doing feature spots, headlining gigs, and other "real" shows, contests seem like a trap. On the one hand, you want to do them to show your dominance. You want everyone to see that you are funnier, a better performer, and that that's why you are getting paid. On the other hand, it's scary, because if you don't win and you are a headliner, it will knock you down a notch or 2. Or 3. Or farther.

The amount of ego in the room of a comedy contest is astounding. I witnessed it myself as a newcomer, and have been guilty of it as a headliner. Nobody wants to lose, yet nobody acts like they care if they win. The mind games are ridiculous. Comedians are not only funny, they are smart and calculating. Being in the green room or meeting room of a comedy contest is one of the most fascinating places I've ever been. Tons of niceties going around, yet internal anger, greed, and egotistical hunger for recognition looming in the air.

I still do them every once in a while, though. I enjoy all that stuff I just said.

The Old City Comedy Competition at Carleo's in the Old City in downtown Knoxville, ran by J.C. Ratliff. The amount of talent in this picture is overwhelming. This is why Knoxville is considered one of the best up and coming cities for Stand Up Comedy in the country.

Festivals

There are all types of festivals that a comedian can be a part of. Obviously, the most well-known is a "Comedy Festival." This can be local, regional, national, and international. Most are regional or national, and will feature comics from many places.

Here in Knoxville, for example, we are about to embark upon our second annual "Scruffy City Comedy Festival." This is a massive gathering of comedians from all over the country, as well as many local and regional comics, in downtown Knoxville. Shows will last for 3 days, in several different venues. Each night, comedians will be placed on different shows at different places, giving the audience a unique line up each time.

There are comedy festivals all over the country. Some are harder than others to get into. As a comedian, you must submit videos, a short bio, and a fee just for consideration. The chances of being accepted are slim unless you are just that good. Yes, I have been turned down several times. I've learned the importance of having a good video for festivals. It matters.

Comedy festivals, however, aren't the only opportunities for comedians to perform in a "festival" setting. There are music festivals, where comics are often asked to perform between bands. There are Variety type festivals, with performers of all types. Really, comics can end up at any kind of festival at any time, any place. It's like that with shows in general. Somehow, we end up finding ourselves in positions we never would have imagined.

All in all, festivals are fun. Period. It's a great way to meet new people, whether they are other comics, performers, or just there. Even when not performing, you have things to do and see, instead of hanging out in a hotel room.

Theaters

This is a tricky one. Traditionally, when you think of a comedian performing in a theater, you think television and thousands of people. Yes, that is definitely the pinnacle. Comedy club and Underground comics alike would agree that is at the top of the list. However, there are other "theater" type shows that can be smaller. Much, much smaller. Yet, they are always special shows. Theaters have a different kind of feel and ambience than a bar or comedy club.

I don't mean to give you a lesson in the aesthetics of a theater, but I think it's important to show the difference. Here's the deal: In a bar, there are people everywhere. At tables, at the bar, walking around, standing in front of the stage, playing pool, playing darts, and dancing. There is so much going on. In a comedy club, people are sitting at tables, in a compact setting around the stage. It is relatively a small place, even when it seats 250 to 400 people. Now, in a theater setting, the people are sitting in rows, sometimes far back to where you can't even see them from the stage. The stage itself is huge, unlike the corner of a bar or a small comedy club stage. You feel like you are floating in an ocean.

I will never pass up the opportunity to perform in a theater. I don't care about the money. It's a feeling that's just impossible to duplicate anywhere else.

Charity Events

Another popular setting that comedians find themselves in are charity events. Any type of charity, it doesn't matter. If you are a comedian, and you are available, then do it. This is the one moment that being on stage isn't about yourself.

99% of the time charity events are clean and family friendly. Yes, this is a big reason many comics don't do them. The other is that you don't get paid. When I was just starting, I didn't really know how to work clean. I was asked to do a charity event, so I had to learn. I didn't hesitate. The fact that I would be able to possibly help raise money for those in need by telling jokes was enough for me. Who cares if I messed up? Who cares if I didn't get paid? It wasn't about me. The feeling you get from performing for charity is different than the rest. If you are a comic and you are reading this, do them. Whenever possible.

Corporate Shows

Ok. This is where it starts getting really interesting. Corporate shows are no holds barred. If you are a comedian who is able to do corporate shows, then you know that predictability is out the window.

Personally, I stumbled into the world of corporate comedy. I wasn't planning on it, but it just happened. I had heard enough horror stories about them to figure out I didn't want to do them. Strange conference rooms. Hundreds of people, usually of the same profession or same company. Not really sure if they want clean or not. Not really sure if they want you to talk about them or not. Not really sure if they want you to be there, even though they are paying you good money. No other comics there. No other friends. Nobody. On an island. By yourself. Pressure. Money, usually more than you are used to for one show. Telling jokes while people eat. And drink. Or don't drink. You never know. Could be a sober G rated show. Could get there and everybody is drunk and wants it dirty. Sometimes the person hiring you is a Human Resources Manager who really isn't sure what you are supposed to do. You just never know.

That's why I love them. All of it. For myself, the unpredictability is the equivalent of a thrill seeker base jumping off a skyscraper. It fascinates me. It motivates me. As you will read later, I've walked into situations that would make you want to throw up. Actually, I think I did that a couple of times. However, it always goes well, I always have fun, and I always earn my money. This is one type of show where you have to be your best, you have to improvise at the last second, and, most importantly, you have to have confidence. You can't walk up to the mic, or podium, and blank out. You can't shake. You can't show weakness. You are getting paid way too much for that.

The Strange Shows

Sometimes, as a comic trying to make it, you end up taking jobs that just don't fit into any of the above categories. Restaurants, boats, alleys, lodges, wine stores, bowling alleys, gymnasiums, backyards, living rooms, and pretty much anywhere else you could imagine. You just never know who wants, or thinks they want, comedy at their place. Out of curiosity, and just pure adventure, I always say yes if I'm available. I've immediately regretted many of these shows as soon as I've arrived at them, yet it usual ends with Jenny and I laughing all the way home.

I've had moments where I've made $1,000 in one week doing theaters or corporate shows, only to follow it up the next week by performing in strange places with the hopes someone will give me $5 as I run to my car. You just never know. It's the opposite of a corporate show. They are both exciting in their own right, but with "strange" shows, you don't even know if you will make a penny. You may even lose money. You may get cussed out and run out of the place. When I said corporate shows were like base jumping off a skyscraper, strange shows can be like actually falling without a parachute and hitting the ground. But, you just laugh them off. That's the only way to handle it. Plus, the experience you gain from them is unmatched. You learn things about yourself and ways to handle tough situations that you didn't think possible.

Don't believe me about the strange shows, huh? Well, this is me, on a flatbed trailer, in an alley. In the background is the audience. I did almost an hour for them.

The next several chapters, I am going to tell you some specific stories. Stories of my most memorable shows from all of the types of "gigs" I just mentioned. Now, I know that I left off "Improv" shows. Unfortunately, I've not had the opportunity to do more than 3 minutes of that, so I can't speak from experience. Improv comics are impressive. Here in Knoxville, we have one of the best Improv groups I've seen, Einstein Simplified. To be able to hit the stage, as a group, and work off the cuff in different scenarios is outside of my repertoire. But, who knows. Maybe one day I will try that too. I've done most everything else.

Oh.... The Bar Shows

Like I said before, Bar shows are some of the craziest and best shows. Here are some of my favorite experiences, from some of my favorite places that I've been over the last 5 years. They weren't all great, but they were definitely all memorable.

Giggles Grill: The Comedy Catch, Chattanooga, TN

As a comedian in the Southeast, there are few places like the Comedy Catch in Chattanooga, TN. The history, the ambience, the intimidation. It has it all. As a newcomer, though, it's not easy to get into the main showroom. The owner, Michael Alfano, is one of the most respected names in the business, and everybody wants to perform there. But first, you would have to show your stuff in their side room, known as Giggles Grill.

My first experience in Giggles Grill was with Sandy and Jay. Sandy had been performing both there and in the main showroom for a while, so he was well acquainted with the layout.

Giggles Grill is the bar area leading to the main show room, similar to the room I started in at Side Splitters in Knoxville. It's bigger though, more like a restaurant. It's situated in a part of town that most would consider unsafe. Brick walls. Small sign. But everybody in the area knows it, and it's why they get the big names. It's the real deal.

Now, over the years, I've been fortunate to have the opportunity to perform in Giggles Grill many times. The stage is situated in the corner of the bar, with large windows on either side. Cars are driving by, as you try to perform to a mixed crowd. Timing, as far as your position in the open mic lineup, was key there. It would take me a while to learn this. If you went too early, the crowd wasn't there. If you went too late, the crowd had left. If you went in the middle, the people arriving for the main showroom were walking in, loudly.

Needless to say, it was unpredictable. As you have probably figured out by now, unless you are in the main showroom of a comedy club, or a theater, comedy is unpredictable. That's just the way is.

One of my first shows in Giggles Grill, 2010. One of my first times actually leaving Knoxville to try comedy. Nervous would be an understatement.

Giggles Grill is where I would make many long-time friends. Some of the best comics I know, such as Corey Forrester, D. J. Lewis, and Jerry Harvey would share the stage there before becoming regulars in the main showroom and other comedy clubs everywhere. The line ups for every open mic there were incredible. I always gave my best there, knowing that I was that close to the main showroom.

There were many memorable nights there. However, there is one that just sticks out like none other.

I very rarely went there without Jay and Sandy, or at least one of them. One particular night, on the drive there, Jay told Sandy and I that he had written 2 new bits he was going to try. He told them to us in the car. Sandy and I both agreed that one of them was great, and the other one was terrible.

Normally, the 3 of us would sit at the same table in the corner, in front of the window. For some reason, on this night we sat in the crowd. There was an older couple sitting next to us. Jay hits the stage, and starts doing his normal thing. Sandy and I are waiting for him to tell the "good" joke he had recited in the car. We knew it was going to be a big one for him, and we were anxious to see it hit the big crowd at Giggles Grill.

Instead, Jay does a 180, and starts telling the bad one. Matter of fact, it was one of the craziest things I've ever heard come out of someone's mouth on stage. Sandy and I didn't know what to do. The older couple next to us quickly grabbed their stuff and left. We were stunned. He never did the good one. He ended it with that horrific joke, infamously nicknamed "The Feared Elves."

Of course, as usual, Jay would walk off the stage, come over to us, and say "boys...I killed it." To this day, he won't admit that he made that older couple next to us leave. At least he never did that bit again.

The Giggles Grill will always hold some of my best memories doing comedy. In late 2015, The Comedy Catch will be moving to a new location downtown Chattanooga. I look forward to performing there soon.

Jay at Giggles Grill. Not sure if this is the same night he told the "Feared Elves" or not. If it is, this picture is worth millions. It only happened once, ever.

Club 1341: Sevierville, TN

I've done a lot of bar shows around the country, and, hands down, this is my favorite place. Yes, this is my hometown. I know. However, they do bar shows in a different way. Oh, and maybe I should mention that this is my own show that I started producing in 2011.

Of course, being a comedian helps when putting together a "comedy" show at a bar. But it takes more than that. Most importantly, the bar owners and operators themselves have to be 100% on board, and they have to *want* to do it.

That is why I love this place. Derrick, the managing partner, and Terry, the owner, listened to my recommendations early on, and every show since, for 3 years, they've expanded on them.

The show started out with myself doing a long set as a local comedian in my hometown. Where I'm from, about 45 minutes from Knoxville, stand-up comedy didn't really exist. It was 2011. It would be my first headlining set. My friend and fellow comic, Dean Jennings, would open for me. I didn't know what to expect. Nobody did, really.

We had a great turnout for the first show. I had planned on doing 45 minutes. I accidentally did about an hour and 15 minutes. I think I was only funny for about 47 minutes. After that, I just rambled. Learned another lesson there.

I did a few more shows there with myself as the headliner before we changed directions. Afraid the locals were getting tired of me, we decided to make it a weekly show, featuring some of the best regional headliners. It would be more similar to a comedy club than a traditional bar show, with an emcee, feature, and headliner, and would be back to back nights to give people a chance to come out. Candle lit tables, all the beer signs and televisions turned off. It was like a comedy club in a bar.

Corey Forrester, D. J. Lewis, Grady Ray, Jamal Gilbert, Riley Fox, Monty Mitchell, Doug Canney, Terry Tee, and other great headliners would come in to perform. Sometimes I would emcee, or feature, or headline. Since it was my show, it was too hard to just sit back and not be a part of it.

My first time getting my name up on a sign. Club 1341 in Sevierville, TN, 2011. One of the best bars to perform comedy in the Southeast.

After a while, the show would fizzle out. We took a break. Then we started doing a show monthly. Then quarterly. Derrick and I were trying to figure out the best way to go about it. Luckily, he and I both have the same vision. There was no doubt we were going to keep it going, and to make it the best show around. When we did it right, we were averaging over a 100 people easily. When I say 100 people at a bar, I don't mean they were "at the bar." I mean they were there to see a show. They quit playing pool. They quit talking. They listened.

Derrick and I at Club 1341. We are either strategizing for the next show, or we are laughing over my tab.

Since 2011, the show is still a success. Over the past year, we have been selective when to do one. When we do, though, it's big. We try to plan our shows on a Saturday night, and with a big named band to bring in the bigger crowds. Most of the time, I work with one of my favorite Tennessee bands, Autumn Reflection. They even let me sing with them, which is a huge mistake on their part, but whatever. It's fun. We advertise, we pack it, and it's a blast. Usually I headline, bringing in different comics every show. It's just one of those venues that continues to get better and better every time. We have big things planned for the future, and I can't wait.

Now, as far as my most "memorable" moment at Club 1341, that's tough. The worst heckler of my life was there, but since this book is PG, I'm just going to leave that out. So, the next memorable moment would be a night that I wasn't even there.

It was 2012. Jenny and I were out of town doing shows at the Comedy Zone in Johnson City, TN for the weekend. I had booked comics at 1341 while I was gone. Matter of fact, it was a co-headliner show with Corey Forrester and D. J. Lewis. Here is the text that Jenny and I woke up to on that Saturday Morning:

"Hey. Just wanted to let you know. D.J. took his clothes off at the show last night and I got into a fight. Talk to you later."

That was it. No details. All I knew is that I was out of town, they got down to their underwear and were fighting the audience.

To this day, they are some of the most requested comics to come back to 1341. And they also keep wanting to come back. I'm not sure exactly what happened that night, but it must have been good all the way around.

Club 1341, in Sevierville, TN, before the crowd rolls in. Candle lit tables, incredible sound system. Great place for comedy.

Here is another thing I love about Club 1341. People come up on stage with you. This is the first night I met Buster Brown, now one of my good friends and best fans. This night could have easily been my most memorable moment there, but, once again, keeping this book PG. Below, Jenny and I at 1341. It's one of her favorite venues.

Preservation Pub: Knoxville, TN

The Upstairs Underground comedy show at Preservation Pub in the historical Market Square is the longest standing open mic in Knoxville. Started by Matt Ward, this show is on the second floor of one of the coolest places in all of Knoxville. Sorry, I couldn't find a better word than "coolest." It just is.

I was fortunate enough to be a part of some of the earliest shows they had there. Sitting on bean bags before the show, right in front of the stage. Taking in the surroundings. The ceiling tiles, the large black and white portraits of famous people like Einstein. One of a kind place.

It's a long bar. From the stage, it's hard to see all the way to the back tables. The bar is situated right in the middle of Market Square in downtown Knoxville. Market Square itself is a place of wonder. Jenny and I spend every second we can there, with or without the kids.

Sandy and I, early 2011, enjoying the large bean bag chairs at Preservation Pub.

The Upstairs Underground Comedy Show at Preservation Pub is every Sunday night. It brings a unique, eclectic crowd. It's a mix of college students and mature, worldly comedy fans. You really have to be on your game to do well there. Sometimes it's packed, sometimes it's a smaller crowd. They listen. They laugh. They stare if you're not funny.

Typically, there are 10 to 15 comics doing 6 minutes or so. Sometimes, there is a headliner to close the show out. My most memorable moment over the last 5 years would be a show like this, and it was not too long ago.

It was February, 2015. My 5 year anniversary of doing comedy. Some will debate this, so let's clear this up. It was my 5 year anniversary of the first night I ever went on a stage. Not my first paid gig anniversary, but the actual first time I touched a microphone. It happened to fall exactly on the night of the Upstairs Underground show. Matt and Boston McCown, who runs the show now, agreed to let me close the show out since it was a special night for me.

I got there early. I was excited. I was discouraged, though, because Jenny couldn't be there because of the kids. She has sacrificed so much over the years coming to my shows, and it was tough to not have her there for this special night.

The crowd was rolling in. It was a big crowd. Packed. People were standing. Many of my friends were there, both performing and watching. They weren't there for me. It was just an open mic. Nobody knew that it was a special night for me. That was fine. It was really just something inside my head.

There was a big line-up that night. I would go last to close out the show, and I was afforded as much time as I wanted. However, it wouldn't turn out to be perfect as I expected.

It wasn't that the comics were doing poorly. It was that the show was going on too long. Everybody was doing so well, time just kept going. One by one, the crowd was leaving. I was laughing. It was typical luck. I just knew that by the time I got up, the only people left would be comics. And, I was right. And, it was perfect.

Boston gives me a great introduction. I stumbled up the big steps to the stage. I had an original set written for a big crowd of people I didn't know. However, as the show went on, and I started to see people leaving, I wrote a brand new set. Just stories. Stories of my stand up life up to that point. I kind of had a feeling that it was just going to be comics watching by the time I got up there, so why not.

I rarely take a piece of paper on stage with me. When I say rarely, I mean never. This was an exception. I had just written this set over the last 2 hours. Not ever jokes. Just random stories to tell.

It's hard to make a room full of comics laugh. Most of the time, they have already heard your stuff anyway, so it's just the same ole same ole. Maybe a new bit or joke here or there, but for the most part, they know what to expect. It's a challenge.

Instead of worrying about being ridiculed for taking a piece of paper up with me, I decided that it was my night, and that I could do whatever I wanted. They all knew I could do an hour anytime I needed to, so I wasn't really worried about it.

I look out into the long bar. The non-comic audience was gone. For all I know, comedians were now the bartenders as well. Many familiar faces, some new. I decided to just let go and have fun. After all, it was my 5th anniversary taking the stage. Why not.

I glanced at the scribbled words on the piece of paper every so often. But I didn't really need them. I was just having fun. I was probably more animated than I had been in a while. Most of it was just stories from my 5 years of crazy shows, that you are reading about now. At one point, I remember glancing over at the wall where the beanbags used to be. I thought about sitting there almost 5 years ago, just daydreaming about doing my own show one day. Who could have imagined the way it actually turned out.

The Bullpen: Alcoa, TN

Where do I even begin with this one? This show was started by Sandy, Jay, and I in late 2010, early 2011. Alcoa is where the Knoxville airport is located. Not too far from Knoxville, and situated in between there and the Smoky Mountains.

The Bullpen was a small place, on a side street. I'm not sure if I ever felt safe there, but it was always fun. There was a dart machine. A bar. Tv's. Smoking. Locals known for fighting for no reason.

When we first started this show, I was still new to the whole comedy scene. I was as far from comfortable in a bar setting as you can get. I hated it. I never wanted to go. I was nervous. If it wasn't for Sandy telling me that it was good for me, and that it would help me in the long run, I would have just stayed home every time. So glad I listened to him.

Sandy knew the owner, Steve, and set it up. We would do open mic style and invite all of our Knoxville comedian friends to come out every week. Every show was interesting. Sometimes it was packed out, and other times there were literally 4 people there. This was by far the most inconsistent show I've ever been associated with, yet I loved it. I never wanted to actually go, but I was always there. It was like a weird relationship.

As far as memorable moments go, the list is long at the Bullpen. If you have seen one of my shows, then you have probably heard of the story of the night where a huge fight broke out, another comic was involved, while simultaneously an infamous terrorist was killed on the television above my head while on stage.

Or, if you have seen one of Jay's shows, you have heard the story about the night he was telling a joke, and got rushed on the stage by a woman who was offended. Definitely one of the most uncomfortable situations I've ever been involved in.

Sandy getting the show started. Jay Pinkerton and Dean Jennings in the background. I'm taking the pic apparently. That was the entire crowd this night at The Bullpen.

The most memorable night, however, would have to be the one where only 6 people were in attendance. That included Steve, the owner, and the bartender. Sorry, I can't remember his or her name, or gender, apparently. There were 4 comics performing that night. Sandy, myself, Nate Cate, and Coley O'dell.

It didn't take long to realize that nobody cared if we did a show. The 4 audience members, plus Steve, and the bartender of no name or gender, really just wanted to drink. We had to do something.

So, we decided to play a game. We let the audience, if you want to call it that, have the opportunity to pick topics, and we would write jokes. The rules were that we had 1 minute to write a joke on whatever topic they picked. We then would perform that joke and let the crowd decide upon the winner. I don't remember all of the topics, but I do remember that we had a blast. It was about as close to improv comedy as I've ever been.

The Bullpen would lead me in a direction that I was hesitant to go. At the time, I thought of myself strictly as a comedy club guy. That was it. I absolutely hated bar shows. I didn't feel comfortable, I was nervous, and I thought it was pointless regarding my comedy goals. I wanted to be a comedy club comic. Period.

However, if it wasn't for The Bullpen, and Sandy, constantly pushing me beyond my comfort zone, I wouldn't be where I am today.

The Thirsty Turtle: Maryville, TN

One of the worst nights of comedy I've ever had. Hands down. Completely my fault.

I had been writing my first book for several months. During that time, I had quit doing shows. I didn't perform at all. For months. One of my best friends, who happens to be a comedian and comedy booker, J.C. Ratliff, asks me to headline a show. Of course, I agree.

Leading up to the show, I had literally spent every minute editing and finishing the book. That's all I cared about. It had probably been 3 months since I had even seen a microphone or a stage. Being the idiot that I am, I agreed to do 45 minutes to an hour at the Thirsty Turtle. At that point, in 2013, I had headlined so many times I thought it would just be easy.

On top of that, I was performing with some of my best friends. J.C. was the host, with J.D. Howard and Jake James Hasenaur opening up. What could go wrong? These guys are like brothers to me. It would be a fun show! Yeah, no.

First of all, as Jenny and I get there, we notice there is a pool tournament going on. Right in front of the stage. The pool tables were literally right in front of the stage, and the crowd was way back. There were a lot of people there, but they were mostly far away, with the pool players in between us.

I scratched this off to the life of being a comedian. Weird situations, odd surroundings. It was nothing new to me. I would deal with it as usual. I kept forgetting, though, that I had not performed in a long time.

J.C., J.D., and Jake do well. I was feeling confident. At least that's what I let Jenny believe. Honestly, I was doubting myself. I had not prepared at all. I was unsure of myself for the first time since I was doing open mics at Side Splitters my first year. I was forgetting my old bits and jokes in my head, and I knew it wasn't going to go well. I wasn't sure how I was going to get through the first 5 minutes, much less 45.

J.C. gives me an awesome introduction as usual. Great. Just great. Now I'm completely doomed. These people, way back in the back of this weird bar, are expecting greatness. And I know I can't give it to them. It was the first time, since I had started doing comedy, that I didn't have that killer attitude. I was honestly scared.

I grab the mic. I look out into the crowd. I blank out. Completely. I don't even know where to start. Something that seemed so easy to me so many times, in so many different places, was now a nightmare. This was the last place on earth I wanted to be at that moment. I was mad at myself for not preparing.

I was terrible. Really, really terrible. It was the first time doing comedy that I just knew it was bad. Now, I'm not going to take all the blame. The cracking of the pool balls in front of me was in my head. The chatter in the back of the room was distracting. No excuses, though. It was my responsibility to perform.

Like I said earlier, my job was to do 45 minutes to an hour. It didn't happen. It's the only time, to this day, that I didn't do the time I was supposed to do. The sad thing is, I would have done 45 minutes if Jenny wouldn't have been sending me the "stop" signal with her hands 28 minutes in. So, that's what I did.

J.C. felt bad. He apologized. But, it wasn't his fault. At all. It was mine. I didn't prepare. I'm a professional. I can deal with any situation, any crowd. That night I learned the most valuable lesson ever. Prepare. Simple as that. Since then, I haven't made that mistake, and I've been in situations much worse than that one.

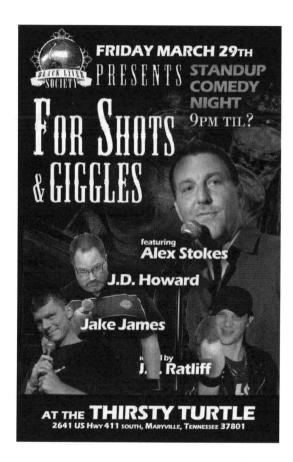

Promo poster for the worst performance of my life. I forgot to mention that there was a Magician performing that night as well, and he basically took over everything. They double booked us. If it was up to him, his face would have been over all of ours on the poster.

Mr. T's Pizza & Ice Cream: Dalton, Ga.

Another one of my favorite spots during my first couple of years. Located on a side road, across from a gravel parking lot in Dalton, GA, Mr. T's Pizza & Ice Cream offered both great crowds and a beer tower.

I can clearly remember that first trip. I only knew the name was Mr. T's, and I had heard that it was a great show. At that point, I had not been to many out of town venues, so I was expecting some really big and grand place.

Mr. T's Pizza & Ice Cream in Dalton, GA. Many great memories at this place.

The first trip was with Jay and Sandy. Matter of fact, I think every trip after was with them too. It was a show we all liked to do regularly. It was a good 2 and a half hour drive from Knoxville, for little money, but it was still fun. Many of the best comics from Knoxville, Chattanooga, and even Nashville on occasion were there. Sometimes from Atlanta. Jerry Harvey from Chattanooga ran the show. When the shows weren't great crowd wise, we still had fun. It was almost like a central meeting place for the region's comics. Good pizza, comfortable atmosphere, and, the beer tower. It was a tower, brought to your table, of beer.

Early poster from Mr. T's. You see, it's a pizza, and the comics were pepperonis. You see? Impressive line-up nonetheless.

Mr. T's was just one of those shows that everyone enjoyed doing. Nothing over the top special. The crowds were good, the comics were always good, the food was good. It was like a well-kept secret hidden off a side road in the carpet capital of Dalton, GA. Jerry Harvey, as always, put together strong line-ups and made it fun. I'd go back there in a second to this day and do a set.

Now, there have been plenty of other shows of memory that took place in bars. Enough to write a book titled "My Life Telling Jokes In Bars." That many. These were just some of my favorites and most memorable.

There is just an excitement of performing in a bar that no other venue has. The adrenaline rush is amazing. It's a real test. There aren't any comedy club bouncers there. The crowd will talk, they will yell, they will play pool and darts. They will heckle, even when they aren't listening from the back of the room. They will walk on the stage, they will grab the mic from you and yell to their friends.

That's part of the challenge, to take control of a rowdy room and make it yours. Once you have learned how to do that, everything else seems easy.

Comedy Clubs

Let's talk about the comedy clubs for a bit. For many, this is where you want to be. My beginning was at Side Splitters Comedy Club in Knoxville, and for the first couple of years, that's where I was destined to end up on a weekly basis. Actually, there is still a good chance that I will end up going in that direction at some point if I want. I absolutely love comedy clubs. Unlike bars, everyone there is actually there to see a comedy show. They want to laugh. There is usually crowd control for those who get a little to rowdy. It's just a different atmosphere, and one that I love.

Before I tell you some of my most memorable moments in comedy clubs, let me explain my position. The following stories are MY stories from my experiences. No, I haven't toured the country performing every weekend at clubs. There are so many, I couldn't really give an accurate description of the ins and outs. I can only base it on my experiences and the clubs I've been fortunate to work in during my 5 short years. I just wanted to clear this up, since many comics are argumentative and always think that the way *they do* it is the only way. Try being friends with hundreds and hundreds of comics on Facebook. It will make your brain hurt.

Side Splitters Comedy Club: Knoxville, TN

I think it was pretty obvious that I would start here. My first open mic. My first feature spot. My first hosting gig. My pictures and newspaper articles on the wall in the lobby. Where I would not only meet Jay and Sandy, but many of my best friends to this day. Yeah, this was my home for a couple years. I lived there when the kids weren't with me. I still drive by the empty building and have wonderful flashbacks.

As you have already read, my crazy comedy ride started here in February of 2010, at an open mic. Over the next couple years, I would spend many nights in Sid's Lounge (the bar area and open mic room) performing 6 minutes of jokes to crowds of 10 or 60. I would also host in the main room for many months for comics from Saturday Night Live, HBO, television, movies, etc. Jay, Sandy and I would have 2 shows of our own in the main room, with one selling out and the other getting close. Contests, charity events, and weekends just watching some of the best in the business and learning. This place was my second home.

In the main show room at Side Splitters in Knoxville. As you can see at the bottom, this picture is from our favorite Knoxville comedy photographer, Tonya Cinnamon. At the time, she was the house photographer for Side Splitters. Matter of fact, many of the pictures of myself are from her. Every comic is excited to see Tonya enter the room, knowing that we will get great shots to use, no matter what the venue is.

The open mics at Side Splitters were always interesting. They would range from 15 to 25 comics. A majority of these would be local regulars, with comics from Nashville, Chattanooga, and Kentucky often coming in. When the crowd was too big for Sid's Lounge, we would move the open mic to the main showroom. It would come in waves. There was an air of excitement when the crowds would start out big an hour before the show. The talk around the room would be if we would get to hit the big stage. We would literally start counting until we hit the magic number.

I literally have so many great moments from the open mics at Side Splitters that I can't recall half of them. A few would be my first night ever on stage, the night I did the 6 minute long joke about a hand turkey, the first night I saw Monty Mitchell from Nashville talk about tacos, the first time I saw Jimmy from Kentucky do his "dicktatorship" joke, Sandy playing the banjo and bombing on purpose, falling off the stage, twice, seeing Barney Young do his dance, Dean Jennings sing his songs, Brad Hinderliter rip an audience to pieces with crowd work...watching Leo Russell mess up the stool before I went up. Just too many to recall. There is one open micer, and I think the rest would all agree, who stood out above the rest. For the right reasons? Probably not. But, he did.

Senor Sexy. Not a care in the world. Dressed in all black. Black hair, thick black mustache. Nicest guy in the world. Had a notebook full of who knows what. One of a kind.

Every Wednesday, we would all sit and wait to see if Senor Sexy was on the list. We would hope so. You see, when Senor Sexy performed, it would be 6 minutes of pure randomness. He had his notebook full of ramblings that he would take on stage. Everybody wanted a peak at what was written in those pages. However, nobody knows what was in that little notebook, and more than likely, he didn't either. He would start reading, then just say "I don't know what's going on. I don't know what I'm saying. I'm out." Then he would walk off stage. He had 6 minutes, but he would often leave at 3. Or 4. Or whenever he felt like it.

The one thing everyone knew was that we would laugh. It was unconventional, it was weird, it was funny. It worked. While we all thought he was just rambling, it wouldn't surprise me to find out one day that he knew exactly what he was doing the whole time. He made the open mics interesting. Senor Sexy is a legend.

Having fun, as always, in Sid's Lounge at Side Splitters Comedy Club in Knoxville. One of the premier open mics in the Southeast.

After the open mics at Side Splitters every Wednesday, the main shows would occur from Thursday through Saturday. There was one show on Thursday, with 2 each both Friday and Saturday. I was fortunate enough in my first year to get my first guest spot for headliner Andy Hendrickson. During my second year, I would become one of the house emcees, getting to share the stage with many greats such as Kevin Meaney, Tracy Smith, James Sibley, April Macie, James Johann, Josh Blue, Gary Gulman, Dale Jones, Darren Carter, Carl LaBove, and Jimmy Schubert.

To be honest, I never liked hosting. However, I knew how the system of climbing the ladder worked, and to be honest, I learned a lot. That's why they do it. It's not an easy job having to warm up a crowd, and many of the above headliners would sell out the weekend. So, overall, the experience was great. Especially the 5 shows each with Kevin Meaney and Josh Blue. The club was electric for each show, with standing ovations afterwards.

One of the perks of hosting...getting to share in special occasions with some of your best fans. Here, I'm helping Side Splitters #1 guest, Wayne Begarly, celebrate his birthday.

Side Splitters will always hold a special place with me. It's where I started. It's what kept me going. The many incredible people I was fortunate to meet and become lifelong friends with. The long nights of hosting 2 shows, learning and honing my skills. The special, fun shows, like Promedy and Halloween. The M.L.C. shows. All of it. Unfortunately, in December of 2014, it closed its doors for good.

Thanks again to the amazing Tonya Cinnamon, for making my time at Side Splitters memorable. She put this together for me.

Hands down. One of my favorite places to perform over the years. Unique is not the right word. Eccentric is not the right word. Unequaled would probably be the best word. Yeah, let's go with that one.

Out Front On Main was a combination of a theater and a club, situated right on the campus of Middle Tennessee State University in Murfreesboro, on the outskirts of Nashville. I put it here, under the comedy club section, because they ran their shows more like a comedy club, with a headliner for 2 or 3 nights straight. Honestly, it could have been categorized as either.

The owner, George W. Manus Jr., will always be one of my favorite people I've had the pleasure to not only work for, but call a friend. He always made me feel welcome, took care of Jenny and I, and packed it out. I was fortunate to headline 3 nights in both 2012 and 2013. Matter of fact, in 2012, I had their first sold out show! I don't know how that happened, but it did! That was an incredible honor.

What a night.

Out Front On Main was an interesting venue. Half of the seating was old Church pews. The other half, movie theater chairs. It also served as a playhouse, so the stage was always filled with props. The green room was a dressing room. There was literally stuff everywhere. But, from Thursday through Saturday, for years, it was a comedy club, with some of the best regional talent hitting that awesome stage.

2 of my favorite people in the world. From left to right, Monty Mitchell, George W. Manus Jr., and myself.

Jenny and I have traveled quite a bit for comedy. Florida, Georgia, North Carolina, and other states all over the southeast. However, this was our favorite trip. We always looked forward to going to Out Front On Main. It was just different. That's really all I can say. The best of the best of Nashville comics would join us for the shows, rotating each night, so we could see and hang out with all of them. So, I'm sorry to say, you are about to get barraged with pictures. I think you already have an understanding that this was one of my favorite places, so there isn't really much more I can say. So, I'll just show you.

Eric Steele, William Langston, Joe Kelley, Irene Bunny Sturtevant, Brad Hinderliter, myself, and Monty Mitchell. There are multiple headliners on that stage, so it was an honor to take that position that night.

Ok, I'll admit. I really like this picture. Like a whole lot. Although, Monty and Brad made changes to it afterwards. Since this book is PG, I won't show what they did. Just a slight rearrangement of the letters, that's all.

What talent in this picture! From left to right: George W. Manus Jr., Myself, Bryce Damuth, Holly Amber, Monty Mitchell, and Peter Depp. One of the best nights ever.

Once again, I'm sorry to say, that Out Front On Main closed its doors. I will miss that place. However, I look forward to getting back to Murfreesboro and the Nashville area very soon, and reuniting with so many amazing people.

The Comedy Catch: Chattanooga, TN

Prestige. Ambience. Atmosphere. History. Yeah, you guessed it. The Comedy Catch. Chattanooga.

I've already told you about Giggles Grill, the bar and open mic at the Comedy Catch. Luckily, on several occasions, I've also been fortunate enough to have been given the opportunity to perform in the main room.

Let me paint a picture for you. As you leave Giggles Grill, you step into a small room. This is where merchandise is sold on the right, restrooms to the left. On the wall, to the left, there are black and white photos of almost every famous comedian you could name. All of them. At this point, you are only a few steps away from entering the main showroom. It is kind of dark. The bar is immediately to the left. The stage is to the immediate right, and it's fairly small. It's surrounded by tables, up close and personal. There is a second layer of tables, then a third in the back. It's intimate, yet big. It's what you would imagine a comedy club to be like. It's musty. It's dimly lit. It's right in your face. It is, in one word, incredible.

Having some fun after a show on the main stage with Jerry Harvey.

Over the years, I've performed on the main stage at The Comedy Catch several times. Showcases, charity events, and just random shows. It's one of those places that when you get the opportunity, you go. Some of my best memories will always be there.

I'm not going to lie. Being a young comic (experience wise) and performing on the main stage was quite intimidating. It had been a little over a year since my first open mic before I got my first opportunity.

My most memorable show there is easy. Very easy.

I had written a new bit. I wasn't sure if it was funny or not, but I liked it. I still like it, even though this particular night is only one of 2 times I've tried it to date.

It involved props. A cowboy hat and lipstick to be exact. I'm not going to tell you what it was about, just in case you come to a show some day and I might surprise you. Here's what it looked like though.

I don't really have any good words to say about this.

Really, all I have to say about that night is this. I dropped the lipstick on the carpet on the stage. I panicked. I put the mic stand over it. After I walked away, I went straight to the bathroom. I started to try to wash all the lipstick off with water. It wasn't working. I was obviously frustrated. Then, from the stall next to me, I hear this burly man say "Hey man. The only way to get all that lipstick off your face is with soap and hot water. Trust me." Then I heard a flush, and saw this huge man in all camouflage walk by. He nodded, and left.

By the way, that whole soap and water thing works.

I'll miss the old Comedy Catch. But I'm looking forward to performing at their new location downtown. When one chapter ends, another one begins.

Zanie's Comedy Club: Nashville, TN

Zanie's Comedy Club near downtown Nashville is one of the premiere comedy clubs in the Southeast. This is where the best of the best headlines.

From the outside, it doesn't look like much. Actually, from the outside, most comedy clubs I've been to don't look like anything special. It's when you get inside...that's when you know.

Zanie's is another intimidating set up for an aspiring comic. The stage, once again, is small, and the audience is right up in your face. There is a green room for the comics immediately to the left of the stage. One thing that makes Zanie's a little different is the balcony. There are people looking down at you while on stage.

I've been lucky to perform there on 2 occasions to date. The first was a showcase, where I was given 15 minutes to do my thing. Some of the best regional comics were also there, and it was a fun show. Jenny went with me, and, as usual, we had a blast. She watched me pace in the parking lot, get nervous in the green room, only to be fine once I got the mic in my hand. That used to be my routine.

My second time performing there was a last minute surprise. I was on Facebook one Saturday morning, and I saw my good friend and Nashville based comic Brad Hinderliter post that he was hosting the Last Comic Standing auditions at Zanie's. I messaged him, jokingly, to see if there were any spots available. He told me to message Lucy Sinsheimer at Zanie's, with a video, and she would see what she could do, no promises though. So, I did.

The next day, on a Sunday morning, Jenny and I were walking around at a food show. My phone buzzes in my pocket. I look, only to see an email stating that I had been accepted to audition for Last Comic Standing. Tuesday night in Nashville. I almost freaked out in the food show! I now had 2 days to prepare!

Unfortunately, due to it being last minute and the whole "we are parents" thing, Jenny couldn't go with me. So, I hopped in the car that Tuesday afternoon and headed for Nashville. As usual, I was really early. Like so early the club wasn't even open. Luckily, Brad and another great Nashville comic, Joe Kelley, were hanging out and playing pool down the street. So, I went and hung out for a while, calming my nerves a little bit. At this point, I didn't know any of the details. I didn't know who else was auditioning. I didn't know the rules, except what was in the email.

After an hour or so, we decide to head to the club. I'm anxious. I'm excited. I can't believe I'm this close to the next step, which was New York. I expected there to be 100 comics there getting an audition. From the seasons I had seen before, they showed lines of comics standing outside getting a chance.

Not this time. There were only 26 comics there. By invitation only. The best of the best from around the Southeast. Mo Alexander, Janet Williams, Monty Mitchell, Dusty Slay, Julie Scoggins, Carmen Morales, and the list goes on.

The first thing I had to do was to fill out this long form for NBC, with my background, career stuff, etc. I was nervous just filling it out. I knew mine was not going to be as extensive as the others. I also knew that I was fortunate to be there, and that I had worked hard to put myself in this position. I was starting to like playing the underdog role.

Pre show with Monty Mitchell. Pretty sure I'm texting Jenny this
"Hey...umm...yeah...well...there are a lot of really good comics here.
Oh, and Monty is being goofy next to me as usual."

We have a brief meeting before the show. The comics are listed in order, and put into groups of 6 or 7 to go into the green room. I was late middle. We each had 3 and half minutes to do our thing. Zanie's was packed. I mean packed. The first time I had been there, it was half full. This was crazy. The stage is compact, and there are people right there almost on the stage. There were judges. I'll admit, I was nervous. I'm ok doing 45 minutes to an hour. 3 and a half minutes? That's tough.

In the green room, I'm sitting in the corner. Nervous. There is a TV in the green room, so you can see what is going on in the showroom. This was my first experience with this. My group was stacked. Just my luck. I'm in there with some of the best headliners in the South. Janet Williams (The Tennessee Tramp), Julie Scoggins, Mo Alexander. Nobody knows me. 3 and half minutes. That's it. I'll be fine. No problem. Or, wait...which 3 and half minutes should I do? I knew it in the car, but now I'm not sure. Ugh. (Yes, I just put "ugh" in a book.)

I hear the host call my name. Yet, I don't move. I'm still sitting. Literally everyone in the green room looks at me "to go!" So, I jump up, open the door, and next thing you know, I'm on the stage in front of 200+. Right there. I'm following the best. I have 3 and a half minutes to make my mark. This is it.

I start off strong. Huge laughter. I resorted to one of my old favorites. One of my bits/jokes that never goes wrong, no matter the venue or the crowd. The second one goes great as well. The third one...yeah, here's the problem.

This was a bit about getting wine in the grocery stores in Tennessee. It always worked. Always. Until I decided, on the car ride to Nashville, that I would change it. Stupid decision.

Halfway through this 1 minute joke, I stumbled. I was conflicted. In my head, I wanted to do the bit as I had already been doing it for months before. But I also started to do it the new way that I had just changed in the car ride there, 3 hours before. I stuttered. I got confused. A split second. Just enough to be noticeable.

Now, I'm not saying I would have made it even without the stumble. I wouldn't have. The other comics were just that good. However, take that mistake out...and I killed it. I was proud of myself. I made the most out of my 3 and half minutes. I felt like I belonged there. I was surrounded by great, great comics.

On the 3 hour car ride home, by myself, I reflected. I smiled. I just performed on one of the most prominent stages in the country. I was competing against the best. I got huge laughs. Yeah, I stumbled on one joke, but who cares. I overcame some fears that night. I just did something unimaginable, at least to myself.

It was a weird feeling. I had headlined many times before. I had opened for many of the best comics out there. I had accomplished a lot already. But, this was different.

As you have probably figured out, I didn't make it to New York. Only 2 comics did. Dusty Slay and Julie Scoggins. They deserved it. They were amazing. I was proud of them, and proud of myself, and I can't wait to get back to Zanie's.

The Comedy Zone: Charlotte, NC

One of the most incredible comedy clubs in the country. No question. I've only been there once. The crowd was small because of snow. But I could tell. When packed, it would be unlike any other club I'd been to. It is not only twice the size as most other clubs, it has that "you made it" feeling. Plus, factor in the "Comedy Zone" name, and it's just for real.

Once again, I was fortunate to get the chance to perform there. I worked hard to get opportunities such as this.

Every month, led by the wonderful Blayr Nias, they have the "Almost Famous Comedy Show." This is where 5 or 6 comics get to show their stuff, like a showcase, with a feature comic to end the night. I was fortunate enough to be the feature this night.

It just so happened that on this night, my good friend Monty Mitchell was also on the show. We decided to meet up and ride together. I should have known that this trip would end up being one of his new stories on stage. Still to this day.

We met in a Bass Pro Shop parking lot in Sevierville. He would drive us the rest of the way to Charlotte, approximately 4 hours away. What a trip this would be.

Halfway there, he remembers that he has something for me in the backseat. Monty and I have a mutual fan from California. Wayne Knisely. Yes, I actually have one fan besides Jenny.

I was lucky enough to share the stage with this group of comics. Just in case you can't read their names: Myself, Spencer Yoo, Kelly Roland, Monty Mitchell, Will Jacobs, and Leo Hodson.

Monty and I arrive, finally, at the Comedy Zone in Charlotte. I think we took a few wrong turns, which were my fault. The snow and traffic being stopped on the mountain didn't help. I'm used to driving and I'm a horrible navigator. Just ask Jenny.

As soon as we get there, we walk into a bar area that is as big as most comedy clubs I'd been to. We navigate down some steps to the showroom. It's massive. It seats 400, almost double the size of Side Splitters back in Knoxville. The stage is big and very centrally located. I was impressed.

Unfortunately, due to the weather, the crowd was very small. Maybe 50 to 60 people. It didn't matter. They packed around the stage, making it a very intimate setting.

The show is structured as a contest. Luckily, on this night, I was the feature at the end and not part of the contest. So, the only pressure I had was to just be funny.

The rest of the trip, well, I'll just leave that to Monty. Go see him perform sometime, and you will probably hear about it.   ~ 137 ~

I look forward to getting back to the Comedy Zone soon, hopefully to a packed house so I can experience and appreciate the full effect of this amazing venue.

There are some other incredible comedy clubs I've been lucky enough to perform at. The Stardome in Birmingham, AL, is one that you will read about it the next chapter.

I will always enjoy performing in a comedy club. It's a different vibe than you get with bars and other venues. It's nice to be on a stage in front of people who are actually there to see comedy.

Contests

Ahhh...the dreaded word amongst aspiring comedians. Contest. Well, let me just say this. We hate them and we love them. We say "I'll never do another contest", then we enter another one on Facebook the next day. Ego. Pure Ego.

There are many variations of comedy contests. The structure can be different, and the judging can vary. You really never know what you are getting into each time you sign up for one. Personally, I've won a couple that I thought I should have lost. I've lost a few that I felt I should have won. Unlike sports, though, there is not a clear cut winner. It's subjective, and it can be tough to deal with, unless you have a level head.

Oh, and yes, I still do them every once in a while. Ego, remember?

Here are a few of my experiences with contests.

The Stardome: Birmingham, AL

So far, in my 5 plus years of doing comedy, I have yet to perform at a place like this. Wow. That is all I can say.

The club, from the outside, is unassuming. Just like many clubs. Even once you enter the doors, you are still unaware that it is a venue like no other. Inside, to the left, is the ticket booth. To the right, a small bar. Straight ahead, a curvy hallway leading to different showrooms. That's all you see.

In 2012, Jay, Sandy and I signed up for an open mic contest there. I didn't really know what was happening. I was still fairly new to the whole comedy thing. I was just enjoying hanging out with Jay and Sandy, learning from them, and having fun. That was it. I was about to get my world rocked, however.

From what I can recall, here is how the contest at The Stardome worked. First, there was a series of qualifier rounds. These were performed in the B room, not the main showroom. At most clubs, the B room is small. At the Stardome, there were 200 people there for the qualifier round. It was packed.

Each qualifier round, 2 comics would advance to the finals, which would battle it out at a later date in the main showroom. On the big stage.

I can remember the qualifying round clearly. The 3 of us show up. We go in the front door, and immediately sit at the bar to the right. We start talking to people, meeting people. Eventually, all of the participating comics are there. We draw numbers. This will be the order in which we perform.

Next, we are escorted through a contorted maze of doors and hallways, to another hallway. This is where we would all wait. The show was beginning. At this point, I had not seen either the B room or the main showroom. Just a bar, doors, and corridors. That's it. I was confused and nervous.

Waiting in this hallway, we could hear bits and pieces of what was going on during the show, but only when the door would swing open. There was a small sound booth in the hallway with us. I had no idea where the stage was, what the room looked like, or how many people were there. We were in the back of the hallway, so everything was unclear to us.

I had been nervous many times before. But this time was different. Prior to this night, at least, I had seen my surroundings. I knew what I was getting into. I knew what was expected. Not this night. I was going in blind.

Sandy goes in first. By this time, we had moved closer to the door. Jay and I couldn't hear Sandy, but we could hear laughter. He was killing it. Seriously killing it. I was next, and Jay was near the end. We were scattered among 15 or so comics, from many different cities from the southeast, and we knew that only 2 would advance.

When my name gets called, I take a deep breath. I had been in contests before. I had performed in large comedy clubs before. I was nervous, mostly, because I didn't even know where I was going. There was a door. That was it. That's all I'd seen. I had zero clue where the stage was or what the room even looked like.

I cautiously walk through the door into a dark, packed room. I make my way in and out of tables to the stage, which luckily was well lit, or I may not have found it.

I get a 10 second intro and it was off to the races. A crowd of a little over 200 in this side room, and they were loving it. I did my 5 or 6 minutes, got plenty of laughs, and left the stage happy. As I walked back through the door to the hallway, and saw the other 15 or so contestants, I wasn't expecting anything. I knew they only selected 2 to advance. I was still satisfied, though, because I knew I had just gone into an uncomfortable situation and performed well. I was learning one performance at a time.

Finally, the show ends, and the emcee goes back onstage to announce the 2 finalists. First, they announce Sandy. Jay and I were not surprised. From what we could hear, he killed it. Then, out of nowhere, I hear my name. I was shocked.

A few months later, we would have to go back to compete in the finals. This time, however, would be much different. This was on the main stage. One of the biggest "main stages" in the country.

We arrive early as usual. We get ushered down the mysterious hallways again, this time leading to a green room. There were 12 finalists, and everyone there was talented.

Right before the show was to start, I snuck out to take a peek at the crowd. I walked back through the maze of hallways, found a side door, and walked onto the upper section. First of all, the place was packed! 400 plus. Second of all, I can see why it has the "dome" part in its title. It's huge, and unlike any other comedy club or venue I had seen up to that point (still to this day, actually.) Lastly, I looked at the stage. It was gigantic, and on top of that, it had jumbotron sized tv's over the stage! Yeah, this was new for me, and now I was really nervous.

I was in the middle of the pack of performers. Sandy was before me, and he did great as always. I was unsure of what jokes and bits to do. It was another short set, around 6 minutes. The winner would get to come back and perform on a weekend for a major headliner. I wanted to win it so bad.

I had recently written a new bit before this show, and had only tried it once. It had worked well, so, at the last minute, I decided to do it again. I put it in the middle of my set, in between proven jokes that I didn't have to worry about.

Well, let's just put it this way. My set was going great, the entire place was laughing hard. Then, the new bit came up, I stumbled on one word, and that was it. I finished well, but that one joke, that one stumble of words, did me in. Everyone else was so good, there was no chance. Sandy would finish in the top 3, and would get an opportunity to come back. Jay and I were so happy for him. This was a great contest, especially for a newcomer like me. I was fortunate to have made it to that second round just to get a chance to perform on that stage. I gained another level of confidence that night.

The Rocky Top Comedy Contest: Knoxville, TN

The Rocky Top Comedy Contest is another event produced and created by Matt Ward. Comics from the Southeast submit a video and short bio, and then wait to be selected. I have been fortunate to have been a participant in 2 of them.

The first Rocky Top Comedy Contest was in 2010, and I somehow squeaked my way into the fray. It was at the Relix Theater, on the outskirts of downtown Knoxville. The Relix was a variety theater, and it had an interesting setup.

At the time of the first contest, I had only been doing comedy for less than 8 months. It was October 2010. It wasn't my first contest, but it was my first competition against out of town comics. Up until that point, I had only competed against Side Splitters friends.

As you can tell, since it's becoming a theme in this book, I was a nervous wreck. I got there extremely early, and Jay and Sandy were with me for support. It was a large place, almost warehouse like. There were rows of benches, like church pews. The stage was large, with a huge white screen in the background. At the time, I didn't know who most of the comics were. It would be a couple of years before I'd figure out they were the real deal.

The first ever Rocky Top Comedy Contest at the Relix Theater in Knoxville. I don't know if you can tell from this picture, but I was a nervous wreck.

Before the show, all the comics went to this strange loft overlooking the stage. We were sitting on couches and random chairs, just waiting. Matt would eventually come up and have us draw numbers. I didn't even want a number. I was scared to death. These guys were from all over, and talking about the shows they had done. I was a nothing. A nobody.

Needless to say, I didn't do that well. I didn't place. Nobody would ever remember my set that night. But, it was a great learning experience. It would prepare me for many situations that were to come.

The second Rocky Top Contest I would enter would be a few years later. November, 2013, at a place called "The Well." It was kind of surreal since it was formerly a place that I used to take clients to years before when I was an Investment Banker. Now, I'm standing up there telling jokes. What a weird life this is.

This contest was stacked. The absolute best of the best comics in the region. Unlike my first attempt as the Rocky Top champion, this one went better. I wasn't a nervous wreck like before. Plus, now I had Jenny to support me. I made it through the first round. The finals would be a special night.

The Well was a neat place. It was literally a door in a strip mall. You open the door, and walk down steep steps to a bar. There were several tables, some bar style table tops, a separate game room, and a corner stage. Very unique place.

The finals would put me against some of the best comics in Tennessee and surrounding states. It was a crowd vote. It was literally going to come down to who brought the most people, and who could steal some of the other votes. Also, in the Rocky Top contest, the comics vote for each other, and the votes count extra. So, you had to be really good to win this thing. You can't just rely on your friends.

I did well. I had a strong set in front of a crowd that was standing room only. Everyone was on that night. It was not an easy vote, to say the least. I like the voting style of the Rocky Top Contest, because it pulls in many factors, unlike many other contests that are strict crowd vote (friends) or strict judge vote.

I didn't win, but that's ok. Jenny was there, and she said I was on that night, so that's good enough. She usually tells me when I don't perform well or don't deserve something. She was honest. She said everyone did great, and it was going to be close.

Joe Kelley, myself, Monty Mitchell (our hilarious host for the evening), and your winner, Matthew Chadourne, at the 2013 Rocky Top Comedy Contest. Funny group of guys right there.

Old City Comedy Contest: Knoxville, TN

The Old City Comedy Contest is a newer competition in Knoxville from my good friend J.C. Ratliff. Held at a very cool bar, Carleo's, in the historic Old City in Knoxville (around the corner from my Underground dancing days), this contest features the best of the best local comics, as well as some heavy hitters from around the state of Tennessee.

To be honest, this is the most relaxed I've ever been in a contest situation. Part of this was due to the atmosphere. Carleo's is a narrow and eclectic bar, with a unique stage. Very friendly staff and owners. Just a place you want to be, comedy or not. Another reason for my calmness would be that by the time I entered this contest, I had already accomplished a lot. So, there wasn't as much pressure. Back to the ego thing, remember? I didn't need to enter this contest. I didn't need to prove anything to myself. But I *wanted* to. For several reasons. My friend J.C. was running it, I enjoyed being around all the comics who were in it, and I simply just wanted to win.

The first round went great. There were 3 judges, right at the base of the stage. The competition was stiff, but I managed to win that night. I had a solid set, and felt really good. I hadn't been on stage much prior to the show, so I was happy that I hadn't lost my edge.

The finals would, once again, put me against a really tough line up. There would be no room for mistakes. The judges were slightly different. I would need to bring my best to win it.

However, instead, I decided to be an idiot.

Remember earlier, while at the Comedy Catch in Chattanooga, I did a new joke while wearing lipstick and a cowboy hat? Remember when I said I only tried it twice? Well, this was the second time I would try it. In a contest final. For shock value.

It backfired.

Needless to say, I strayed away from my normal strong set, and decided to do something out of the norm, just to surprise the crowd. Apparently I forgot that there were judges there, who didn't know me. For all I know, they still think I'm a prop comic who wears a cowboy hat and lipstick at every show. And isn't funny.

Because I was definitely not funny that night.

Totally blew it.

I still had fun, though. I was with my friends, making people laugh. You see, contests, while competitive, are still fun. For the most part, everyone is rooting for each other, at least in Knoxville. I can't speak for other cities. Here, we appreciate when one of us has a good night. We recognize it. Most of us don't pout in the alley after we lose. It's a true comedy family. (Don't ask Jenny about this, she will probably say I pout a lot on the car ride home every time.)

Myself at Carleo's in the Old City, Knoxville. Great venue for Comedy or whatever you are in the mood for.

Other Contests I've Been In

During my early days at Side Splitters, it seemed like I was in a contest every month. There was the Opportunity Knox contests, Knox Vegas To Las Vegas, Halloween and Christmas contests. There were many. I usually did well, even though I was new to the whole thing.

One contest that I remember clearly, though, was called "Stand Up & Represent." This was a 2 part contest. First, I had to win a preliminary round to be on the "Knoxville" team. Once I won that, I would become a part of Team Knoxville, along with Grady Ray, James "Papa J" Cook, and Terry Wright. We would then have competitions against the team from Nashville, then Chattanooga, both home and away. Sandy would fill in at Chattanooga for Terry. Being a basketball player all my life, and with a built in competitive nature, I would have to say that these were some of the most exciting shows I've ever been a part of.

We beat Nashville at our place. We beat Chattanooga at our place.
I'm not going to say what happened at Chattanooga.

So, as you can see, not all comedy contests have to be awful experiences. They can be fun. You just have to go in with the right mindset, that's all. Leave the ego at the door, and all will be fine.

Festivals

Quite the opposite of the dreaded "contest", festivals are what they sound like. Festive. Fun. These are like vacations for comedians. A chance to get away from the grind, whether that's weekly shows traveling in comedy clubs, nightly bar shows, or holding down a full time regular job and sporadically doing shows here or there. No matter what, a festival is a break from the norm and a chance to hang out, talk, and be funny without all the pressure.

As I mentioned earlier, comedians aren't limited to comedy festivals only. We perform at music festivals, variety festivals with performers of all types, or any type of festival that has the word festival in it. It really doesn't matter. Obviously, the most common are comedy related.

Here are some of my favorite memories from performing at a festival.

Funny Farm Music And Arts Festival: Greeneville, TN

Technically, this was my second festival of any type. It was set up as an outdoor music festival, specifically rock bands. Greeneville is roughly an hour and a half outside of Knoxville. They wanted a couple of comedians to perform some 20 minute sets in between bands.

Somehow, Grady Ray and myself got the call. Here comes another adventure.

Jenny and I hopped in the car and headed to Greeneville. When we arrive, we find a sign at a little gravel and dirt backroad leading to the festival. We drive through a field, finally parking the KIA in the grass. We have no idea what we are getting into. We walked around a bit, meeting a few people here and there. It was raining, so the crowd turnout wasn't that big. We cross a creek where there were several people drinking beers over a large metal garbage can. Where in the world were we? Yeah, Jenny just gave me that look of "What have you gotten us into now?" I would continue to get that look many, many times over the years. (Still do, quite often.)

We finally get to the stage, which, I must say, was pretty big. It faced a field big enough for Woodstock. It was huge! I don't know how many people they were planning for, but my guess was 200,000. At the other end of the field, probably 200 yards or so, were a couple vendors and food trucks. So far, not many people. Actually, the only people we saw were drinking beer near the creek. We were laughing, as usual.

Jenny and I at the Funny Farm Festival in Greeneville, TN.

People finally started rolling in. Like 20 or 30. Bands started playing. We finally see Grady. He and I look at each other like "Ummm....yeah....ok. Well, let's do this."

Looking into a pasture the size of 2 football fields with only 20 teenage kids standing there waiting to hear the next band is a weird feeling. It's even weirder when you realize that you have to entertain them for 20 minutes. To make it even more interesting, while I'm on stage and in the middle of my set, the next band starts practicing behind me. Drums mostly. I finally had to ask them to stop for a minute so I could hit a punchline. It was stange. Very strange. However, the few people there were still laughing while standing in the rain. Grady did well as always. We all left, chalking it up to another comedy experience.

All in all, it was fun. We always have fun, no matter what. That's our job.

My first ever lanyard as something other than a banker at a convention. It's ridiculous as to how excited I was about this.

The Boro Fondo Festival: Murfreesboro, TN

First of all, I have to say this. Jenny and I love to say the words "Boro Fondo." Like, a lot.

So, this was another unique festival at the historic downtown in Murfreesboro, TN. It was a bicycle, artsy festival with comedians and poets and others scattered among different coffee houses, bars, and art galleries. Many of our friends were there from the Nashville area, so it was going to be fun no matter what.

We all met up at Out Front On Main under the one and only George W. Manus Jr.'s direction. Nobody really had a clue what was going on, who was performing where, etc. It was kind of exciting to be honest. Groups of 15 comedians, spouses and friends, running the streets around a courthouse trying to figure out where to go. It was like a bunch of 4th grade kids on a field trip. Nothing was open, we were all hungry. We were all eating gas station food, standing around outside random store fronts, and laughing.

Finally, we find out we are doing a show in an art gallery. We get there, and it's empty. There is literally nobody there. Not even the owner. I can't remember who let us in, but we all just hung out looking at art for a while. There was no sound system, mic, or chairs. After about a half hour, they finally show up with all the stuff. By this time, Jenny and I weren't feeling well (probably the gas station food.)

Jenny was literally lying down in the car in front of the art gallery. I was dreading even performing at this point. So, I asked to go on early and to cut my set short. I hated to leave but we were both feeling so bad.

Besides the "sickness" part, we had a blast. Just like at any festival, it was a time to hangout without the pressure, have fun, and escape real life. If they ever decide to invite us back to Boro Fondo, Jenny and I will be there in a heartbeat. And not eat at the gas station.

Performing sick in an art gallery. I think I broke the lamp and possibly the mic. I can't remember. Ahhh.....Boro Fondo.

Wallypalooza: Alcoa, TN

Oh, Wallypalooza. Now, this could easily go in the later chapter of "The Top 3 Weirdest Shows", but I'll just tell the story here. I've had so many weird ones, who's counting anyway.

Wallypalooza was a rock music festival first and foremost, with comedians in between bands. Created and produced by Wally Miles, with help from Waylon Whiskey to book the comedians, Wallypalooza happened in a multi room bar in Maryville, TN, not too far from Knoxville.

I remember getting there, after passing it up 3 times, and pulling the KIA into a packed parking lot. I walked in to the main room, where there was heavy drinking already occurring. I had no idea of what I was getting myself into. I had several friends performing that night with me, including Waylon Whiskey, Drew Whitney Morgan, Matt Ward, Michael Dougherty, Grady Ray and Trae Crowder.

I didn't know too many of the bands or band members that were performing that night. Mainly, I remember wandering around this bar, sometimes to the outside patio, trying to figure out what material to do. I was trying to gauge the crowd, but it was hard. It was extremely diverse. For such a random spot, seemingly out in the middle of nowhere, Wally had done an amazing job of marketing. The place was hopping, people everywhere.

This was also during my "nervous" phase. I wasn't too far removed from my first open mic at this point. This was also one of my first shows without Jay and Sandy being there. There were people everywhere. Bands, fans, comics. It was crazy.

When I hit the stage, I felt ready. Well, at least until I looked into the crowd. One of the headlining bands, Crome Molly, was sitting in the front row watching me before they performed. Here's the thing...they wear masks. I couldn't tell if they were laughing or not! It made me paranoid. I kept looking at them. Waiting. For something. I got nothing, except the occasional head nod. It wasn't as much creepy as frustrating. All I wanted was to know if they thought it was funny. I guess I'll never know.

After my set, I went out onto the extremely crowded balcony. I was so confused. I had no idea what just happened. For the first time, I didn't know if I was funny or not. On top of that, I had written a specific bit that I was proud of, only to be outdone by Drew Whitney Morgan that night with a similar bit. Neither of us planned it...it just happened, and his was better. I haven't done it since.

Crome Molly. You see, how could you tell if they were laughing or not? I know I couldn't. Wallypalooza, 2012.

Scruffy City Comedy Festival: Knoxville, TN

I saved the only true comedy festival that I've been a part of for last. The Scruffy City Comedy Festival in Knoxville is the creation of Matt Ward, who is also the brain child of the Cape Fear Comedy Festival in Wilmington, NC, which has been attracting some of the nation's best comics for years. 2014 was the first year for Scruffy City, and it was a huge success. By the time this book is released, the second annual Scruffy City Comedy Festival will be over.

Many people may not realize this, especially with the recent closing of Side Splitters Comedy Club, but Knoxville is one of the strongest and most thriving comedy scenes in the United States. Even without a true "comedy club", Knoxville's stand-up comedy community, as well as it's improv scene, are as good as it gets. So, it was only fitting that Matt would start a comedy festival here.

As with most comedy festivals, to be accepted, you must submit a video. The video is very important. 5 to 10 minutes long is the norm, and it must be from the beginning of a set without editing. I was fortunate enough to have been accepted for both the 2014 and upcoming 2015 festivals.

For 2014, the festival was at different bars and venues, both in Knoxville's historic Old City and Market Square. Comedians from literally all over the country would come. New York, Chicago, L.A., Florida, North Carolina. It was crazy. The schedule ran from Friday through Sunday, and most comics got 2 or 3 different shows over that span.

My particular schedule would put me on Gay St, the main street in downtown Knoxville, in a bar called the Jack Cellar, 2 nights in a row. I also would get to perform in a specialty roast in the Old City at the Pilot Light.

The first night, when Jenny and I arrived (kid free weekend, woohoo!), we were greeted with our lanyards and free drink tickets. Many of my out of town friends, as well as comics I knew from Facebook were there and already having a good time. From the moment we arrived, Jenny and I both knew it was going to be a festive weekend!

My first two shows would be at a bar called the Jack Cellar, right in the middle of downtown. It was connected with a sports bar, with a long, dark staircase leading down to where I would perform. It was a whiskey themed bar, with incredible ambience, and a stage centered in the room. The lighting was great, the sound was great, the audience layout was great. Unfortunately, they have already closed. That seems to be a theme with me, huh?

Being the first comedy festival of its kind in Knoxville, I was unsure as to how big the turnout would be for the shows. Well, I quickly learned that it would be much bigger than anticipated. The Jack Cellar was absolutely packed both nights, with standing room only! The diversity of the comics for each show also made the entire experience unique, both for the audience and the comics.

Myself at the Scruffy City Comedy Festival, 2014. I'm not sure what I was talking about here, but it must have been important.

My last show was a new experience for me. My first roast. Now, this wasn't just an ordinary roast. No, this was the roast of Superman, and I was to pick a superhero and play the part.

I had no idea what to expect. The line-up was stacked, with some of the best comics around. On top of that, most of them had experience doing roasts. So, I was a bit tentative about the whole situation.

To make things even more awkward, I'm not exactly skilled when it comes to making outfits. I had chosen to be Aquaman. Yeah, I know. To be honest, I'm not really sure if anybody knew who I was supposed to be once I put on my costume, if you even want to call what I was wearing a costume.

Don't' ask. Seriously. Just don't.

Being that it was my first roast, and especially on a subject that I wasn't exactly proficient in, the amount of preparation I had to do was more than what I was accustomed to. I had to engage many of my "superhero" knowledgeable friends for advice. I had to move away from my normal story telling style to a short and brash, attack style of comedy. I was out of my element, but I was determined to do well.

The Pilot Light is a smaller venue, but it has an intensity and uniqueness that most other bars don't' have. The lighting and layout bring the audience right to the stage, and the color schemes and overall surroundings make you feel like you are in some artsy theater rather than just a bar.

The roast itself was fun. Not only had I not participated in one before, I had never even been to one. They have them often in Knoxville, yet I just kept missing them. I now see why they do them. They are fun, exciting, and different from the norm of just preparing a set and making the audience laugh. Everyone is involved, and you never really know what's coming next.

Overall, the Scruffy City Comedy Festival was a blast. I can't wait for the next one, and many more to come. Even if I'm not performing, I will still be there to mingle and meet some of the best up and coming comics in the country. I can definitely see the festival growing bigger and bigger over the years, and I'm proud to have been a part of the beginning.

Theaters

I haven't had a ton of experience in theaters, but there are a few of note. Theaters can range from the large, seating over a 1,000 or more, to the small community theaters, sometimes holding less than 100 people at full capacity.

I have been fortunate to have experienced both ends and some in between. The level of excitement when performing in a theater is on another level compared to the bars and comedy clubs. Here are some of my favorite stories.

The Flying Monkey Theatre: Huntsville, AL

When I got booked to perform at The Epic Comedy Hour by Tim Kelly in Huntsville, AL, the only thing I had heard was that it was an awesome show. It was set up more like a showcase, with seven comics doing 10 to 15 minute sets. This is quite different from an open mic setting, where you may see upwards of 20 comics doing 6 minutes each.

As Jenny and I pull into Huntsville, our GPS takes us to what appears to be an old textile mill of some sort. It was a huge building, kind of by itself, and very unassuming from the outside. Once again, she looked at me and said "Here we go again. Another weird show."

Well, we were wrong this time. It would be awhile before we would realize how great the show was going to be, however. As we walked in this ginormous building, we immediately got lost. You see, as usual, I made us arrive very early. It was at least an hour to an hour and a half before the show, so there were very few people there. Finally, we get directions to the theater, which was upstairs.

As we come off the elevator, all we see, in both directions, are small, independently owned business, almost like a flea market. It was huge! Like a football field full of unique and interesting shops. Art, retro clothing, unusual home décor. At the end, to the left, there were double doors. The Flying Monkey Theatre.

We go to the theater, open the doors (not expecting much), only to see this extremely wide room, with over 200 hundred seats. Folding chairs all the way to the back. It had a large stage, and just felt different from anything I had experienced before. It was still an hour before show time, and there was nobody there. I didn't expect much. It was a huge theater, in a renovated factory, in the middle of nowhere, in Huntsville, AL.

Jenny and I find someone and get checked in. They led us through the theater to a green room behind the stage. By far, the most interesting green room I had ever seen. It was a huge, open room, with couches and props for plays and other theater performances. We come to learn that this old textile mill was actually one of the largest centers for the arts in the country, including music, art studios, restaurants, and much more.

We hang out in the green room for a half hour or so, with some comics that we already knew and some that we just met. I ask about setting up a merchandise table for my first book, and they take us back to the front table, right where the double doors were. As we turn the corner, we see a line the entire length of the building waiting to get in. At $7 a person. It was crazy. I'd never seen anything like it.

By the time the show was to start, it was a complete sellout. Standing room only. Over 250 if I remember correctly. They literally turned people away. Jenny and I were amazed. We had success with our own shows back home, but nothing like this. They knew exactly how to do it in Huntsville!

The show was great. We each did around 15 minutes in front of an electric crowd. They were definitely there for comedy. Afterwards, I quickly ran to the lobby to sell and sign books, which sold out pretty quickly. It was a great night, and I can't wait to go back to the Flying Monkey in the near future.

The poster from the Flying Monkey Theater in Huntsville, AL. What a show.

The Rocky Top Playhouse: Sevierville, TN

Well, I have 3 memorable experiences at the Rocky Top Theater/Playhouse in Sevierville. My first Feature spot, a headlining show, and a co-headlining show with the M.L.C. Comedians.

The Rocky Top Theater was a small venue in a strip mall. Very unassuming from the outside, but magnificent once you broke through the small lobby. Only seating around 90 people, and with a small yet comfortable stage, The Rocky Top was one of my favorite places to perform while it lasted. Oh, and it's one of the only "alcohol free" places I've ever told jokes in, so that makes it unique on its own.

My first time there was a last minute feature spot for Michael Palascak, one of the top current comedians today. At the time, Side Splitters in Knoxville had started booking their headliners to perform a Wednesday night show at Rocky Top, before doing the normal Thursday through Saturday shows in Knoxville at Side Splitters.

I had not been doing comedy very long, only around a year at this point, and my longest set to date had been 15 minutes, R rated. However, I was from Sevierville, and had been working hard to move up the ranks. So, when a feature was needed, I got the call. I was asked to do 20 to 25 minutes, fairly clean, and I only had a few days to prepare. Needless to say, I was nervous.

Michael was very nice and easy to work with. It was my first "green room", so I didn't know how to act. I felt like I needed to demand a fruit tray or something, but I didn't. I think I did get a bottle of water and a candy bar. I don't remember. I may have even paid for them.

My dad and stepmother came, and I'm also pretty sure that most of the crowd consisted of my friends. It was my first big show, Michael was from TV, and I was in my hometown. It was a great night, and I somehow pulled off 26 minutes of PG-13. I know this because I have the video.

After that show, the owners of the Rocky Top Theater would ask me to come back and headline my own show. What??? Headline? Well, of course, I agreed. It was my city. I was trying my best to make my way up the ladder.

Once again, another great show. Sold out. Albeit, only 90 people or so, but it sold out. I did 45 minutes. Yes, I was nervous. But, it turned out to be one of the best experiences I've had to date. I learned a lot that night. I did some things right, did many things wrong, and worked my way through it. It would be a huge stepping stone going forward. Plus, I think I got 2 free bottles of water that night in the green room. I think.

Headlining at the Rocky Top Theater in Sevierville, TN. I probably had no business headlining anything at that point, but I did it anyway.

The last show I would do there, before they closed their doors for good (again, I closed down another venue), would be with Sandy and Jay. The M.L.C. Comedians headline the Rocky Top Playhouse. This would be an experience.

At the time of the show, Side Splitters still had a contract with Rocky Top and was sending headliners to do the Wednesday show. This particular Wednesday, we would be the headliners.

We get there quite early, and hangout in our cars in the back parking lot. The theater wasn't even open yet, that's how early we were. We finally go in, hang out in the green room for a while, and wait for the crowd. Once again, it was full.

The stage had props on it from one of the many plays that they had there on a regular basis. Rocking chairs, a small wooden house, etc. Since Sevierville was my hometown, Jay and Sandy decided to let me close out the show. I think they were setting me up.

Sandy and Jay, from left to right, sitting on the stage, watching me perform at the Rocky Top Theater. I'm glad they found this funny. Or not, according to their facial expressions.

Without going into details, we somehow got into trouble that night. We actually didn't do anything wrong, but there were many misunderstandings. Like I said, I'm not going to say anything here, but maybe if you come to a show, you will hear the funny version of the story.

I owe a lot of my growing experiences to the Rocky Top Playhouse/Theater. 3 of my most memorable shows were there, over a span of a year. My first feature spot, one of my first headlining spots, and the first 3 sober crowds. Experience. 100%.

Clayton Center For The Arts: Maryville, TN: Jon Reep Show

Talk about being lucky. Or being in the right place at the right time. Or probably just lucky. The biggest show I've had to date happened because of some weird, unexpected, and extremely short circumstances.

It was a normal Thursday. May 1, 2014. Jenny and I were sitting in our living room, pricing things for a yard sale for the following morning. I clearly remember, I was holding a pair of shoes in my hand, with a $3 sticker ready.

I had my laptop in front of me. After placing the sticker on the shoes, I check Facebook. I see a post about Jon Reep coming the next day. At this point, I only know he's coming to the area, but not Side Splitters, where he usually came.

The post says something to the effect of "Jon Reep needs a feature for tomorrow. Who's interested and available?" I turn to Jenny and say "Honey...Jon Reep is coming this way tomorrow and needs a feature. Should I send him an email or something?" She gives me a stupid look that said "Yes, you idiot."

So, I sent him an email. I knew every other comic in the area was doing the same thing. They were also commenting on his post. There are a lot of comics in the area, I was late getting in on the game, so I knew my chances were slim to none.

I went back to pricing items for the yard sale. Kid's clothes, blenders, old VHS tapes, etc.

About an hour later, I get an email from Jon. I was selected to open for him, the next night!

I was told to be at the Clayton Center For The Arts in Maryville that Friday night. I didn't know what that was, and I had been to Maryville a thousand times in my life. Only 35 minutes away from my house. I had to perform 25 to 30 minutes, PG-13. Oh, PG-13...scariest 2 letters and a hyphen and 2 numbers there is.

I immediately threw down my stack of yard sale stickers, grabbed my notebook, and told Jenny that I had to go work on a set. In the driveway. I would spend the next several hours in the driveway, pacing. I would also wake up the next morning, cancel the yard sale, and spend several more hours in the driveway pacing. This was a big deal. How big? I had no idea.

I call my family and friends to tell them the news. Come to find out, my oldest son, Weston, already had tickets to go see him! He had never seen me perform, and he was going with a few friends, so my level of nervousness went way up!

Still unsure of what I was getting into, Jenny and I stop at a highly spoken of Cuban restaurant, The Aroma Café, on the way to the show. One of the many things that bond us together...good food. It was amazing! While eating, I was nervous. I was having a hard time enjoying myself. Luckily, as usual, she was there with me to calm my nerves. If I had known what was about to happen, I wouldn't have been able to eat a single bite of that incredible food.

We finally pull into the Clayton Center For The Arts. There are several guys directing traffic. I'm confused. How many people are there?? I tell one of the guys that I'm the opening act. He directs me to the back of this huge building, situated at the Maryville College campus. 25 years earlier, I was there for basketball camp. Now, here I am, opening for Jon Reep doing stand-up comedy. Weird. Feeling.

We park the KIA. She gives me a big smile. I think she knows this is a big deal. I'm still in shock a little. I went from a yard sale to this. In 24 hours. We get out of the car, only to be greeted by a bodyguard. What? I had a bodyguard?

He leads us into the back door, and to our green room. It was a 3 room green room, with a private bathroom. Jon wasn't there yet, so Jenny and I decided to walk out on the stage and check out our surroundings.

5 minutes later, I was scared to death. This was not what I imagined.

Jenny and I trying to figure out how to take a picture in the green room. Apparently multiple people had cameras, although we were alone.

We come in on the back side of the stage. It was huge. Like, what you see on television huge. I asked how many people it accommodated. He said almost 1,200. I asked how many people were coming. He said "close to that." I did a quick sound check. I then went back to the green room, with Jenny, and wanted to throw up.

After a while, I got to meet Jon. Super nice guy. We then met with the director of the theater. I asked what PG-13 was. I wanted to be sure what I had written was ok. PG-13 means a lot of different things to different people. PG is easy. R is easy. G is easy. PG-13 is just plain scary.

Luckily, I was good to go.

Then I find out the emcee for the evening was Phil Jarnigan. Whew! A local celebrity himself, who I am friends with. I know I will get a good introduction. That helps calm my nerves. A little.

Phil goes up, and talks me up even more than I expected. I was happy but at the same time the pressure hit. However, this is what I had worked so hard for up to this point. I was ready.

I did it. 29 minutes of PG-13 for over 1,000 people, including my son and his friends. The place was huge. It was glamourous. It was insane. I had never experienced anything like it. Still haven't since. One of a kind night, that's for sure.

I introduce Jon. He comes up, does his thing, and kills it. While he's up, I'm bouncing back and forth from the green room to backstage. I'm not sure what I'm supposed to be doing. I was so excited, anxious, and overjoyed. I had never wanted to do a set so much, and also wanted it to be over at the same time.

As soon as he gets done, I have to go back on stage to do the closing remarks. I get done, walk off, and I'm quickly rushed off to a long hallway with Jon, leading to the main lobby. At this point, I had totally forgotten that I had written a book, and that people might actually be waiting to buy it.

The doors open to the lobby, and we are ushered out to a crowd of people, all waiting in lines, to purchase Jon's cd's. He has a table set up with security all around. I look over, and next to his table, is another table. It's my books. Jenny is sitting there, waiting on me. There are security guards all around. I'll admit, that was pretty cool.

*Signing a book, surrounded by security. I don't know if the guy felt
bad for me or not and bought a book. Either way, I sold out that
night, so maybe they all felt bad for me.*

Fortunately, with only having a day's notice, I had a good amount
of books in stock. I usually don't. I've had many proud moments in
my life, however, seeing my son walk out of the theater to see me
signing books was at the top of the list. Jenny as well. Up until that
point, I think everyone I knew thought that it was just a dream that I
was living. This night, though, I felt like it was all paying off. It was
incredible. Get ready, here come some more pictures from that night.

Just let me have this moment.

Jenny and I finally pack up our stuff after everyone had left. We go back to Jon's room, which was huge by the way. We talk for a few minutes. We walk to the KIA.

I think I just sat there for a while. Jenny just smiled. She let me have my moment. Excitement combined with relief. I just went from preparing for a yard sale to the biggest show of my life in 24 hours.

I was overwhelmed with emotion.

I wanted to sleep, laugh, and cry. I really wasn't sure I should drive.

I still have those $3 shoes, by the way, in case anybody wants them.

Jon Reep and I after the show.

Charity Events

Like I said before, I will always do a charity event if I'm available. Whether it's raising money for children, disease, a kid's basketball team, whatever. The mere fact that my ability to make people laugh could possibly raise money for those in need is good enough for me. I've been a part of so many charity events, I couldn't possibly tell about them all. Here are a few of note.

Chattanooga Locomotion Benefit: Comedy Catch, Chattanooga, TN

This was my first charity benefit show. The Chattanooga Locomotion was a women's professional football team, and the show was to raise money for their expenses. The notorius Comedy Catch would be the host, and the line-up of comedians was stacked! Myself, Jerry Harvey, Kristine Kinsey, Jay Pinkerton, Sandy Goddard, and Grady Ray would spend a couple of hours entertaining both the entire women's football team and the many supporters who came out for the show.

To this day, this has been the only R rated charity event I've been a part of. It was also my first time performing on the main stage at the Comedy Catch. This is also the night I decided to do the lipstick and cowboy hat bit. You've already seen the picture, and I'm not going to torture your eyes with that again.

This was my first taste of being a person who could make people laugh while helping others. It was a wonderful feeling. I remember after the show, as we were all lined up in the hallway shaking hands and greeting the crowd as they left, that every single woman who played on the Locomotion team thanked us. I'll never forget that.

The Zipperheads Comedy Benefit for Conquer Chiari: SideSplitters: Knoxville, Tn

Now, this was a star studded event! At least for Knoxville. The Zipperheads Comedy show was a benefit helping to raise money to battle Chiari, a condition that affects the brain. It was held at Side Splitters Comedy club in Knoxville, and would feature the biggest names in Knoxville media. Radio hosts, television personalities, etc. They would perform stand up, to a huge crowd, with Jay, Sandy and myself performing in between. It was definitely one of the most interesting nights of comedy I've ever been a part of!

Before the show, collaborating with 2 of the finest men in Knoxville. To the left, Attorney Stephen A. Burroughs, myself in the middle, and Mike Howard to the right.

It was an honor that Jay, Sandy and myself were asked to be a part of this grand event. I'm sure there were nerves on both sides. For the 3 of us, we were worried that the media personalities would be funnier than us. Not to mention Stephen A. Burroughs, the host for the evening, who had just taken Knoxville by storm with a legendary media campaign himself. On the other side, I'm betting that the media guys were worried that they couldn't compete with us. Ok, maybe they didn't think that. I was just dreaming that maybe they did.

All in all, it was a wonderful night. Lots of laughter, money raised, and I met many new friends. This was also one of the first shows Jenny attended with me. Hopefully, someday soon, we can do another event like this.

Tons of talent on that stage. Zipperheads Comedy benefit for Conquer Chiari.

Evening Of Elegance: Sevierville, TN

Up to this point, the largest crowd I had performed in front of was 400 people. I was about to nearly double that. In a tuxedo.

The Evening Of Elegance, which is a black tie fundraising dinner for the Dr. Robert F. Thomas Foundation, supporting the medical needs for the residents of Sevier County, my hometown, is a huge event. Dolly Parton is the honorary chairperson, and more than 700 people attended that night.

Amy Woods is the person who booked me for this incredible evening. Her husband, Gary Woods, helped design the cover of my first book, Messing With Tourists. He did the photography and put it all together for me. It was great timing that all of that had come together.

I had never experienced anything like this. It was held at the Sevierville Convention Center. It's a huge place, and everything was set up as elegantly as you could possibly imagine. I recognized many familiar faces since I had grown up there, making me a tad bit more nervous than I already was. Luckily, as usual, Jenny was there to keep me focused and sane.

I only had to do 20 minutes or so, PG, while everyone was eating. Normally, doing comedy while people are eating is a tough task. However, this place was so big, that it really didn't matter. I was able to focus on the entire room, do my thing, and make people laugh. Ok, so, I couldn't tell if the people all the way in the back were laughing or not, but I know the front tables were.

Not long before it was my time to go up, I kissed Jenny, and left here alone at a table in the back. I wasn't too concerned. She had great food and wine to keep her busy.

On my way to the stage, I got lost, and ended up behind a curtain with the kitchen employees. After telling them who I was, they directed me to the stage, and everything was good.

I took a deep breath. Smiled. This is what I loved to do, only this was on a bigger platform than what I was used to. I wasn't worried that I wouldn't be good. My main concern was falling off the enormous stage. Luckily, that didn't happen. What a night. A true Evening Of Elegance, that's for sure.

Jenny made me pose for this picture. Evening Of Elegance. What a night.

Corporate Shows

It's time to enter the world of unpredictability. Personally, corporate shows are at the top of my list of most favorite shows to perform at. I know many of my friends' cringe at the thought, but for me, it's my version of rock climbing. It's a rush. It's always different. Most of the time, I don't know what I'm walking into until I get there.

I'll admit, yes, the money is good at corporate shows. Honestly, at some point in my life, I could easily see myself being a full time corporate comedian. I love it.

Here's my experience with this type of show. I get an email or phone call from a Human Resources manager. They tell me that they've decided to try a comedian this year for their Christmas party, and that someone told them I was good. We negotiate a price. I get few details.

A few months later, I put on a nice outfit, hop in my car, drive to a nice hotel conference room or restaurant, to perform for a specific group of people, usually in the hundreds. Like I said, the money is good. The pressure is high. The perks, like food and wine, are amazing. It's a good gig, and, I'm good at it.

This is where being flexible with material is a huge positive. I can do an hour G, PG, or R, or a combination of it all. I can do whatever they want. I can switch at the last minute. Many times, they don't know what they want until you get there. Sometimes they will tell you, at the last second, that you should do specific jokes about specific topics. It's my own private improv show in my head.

Here are some of the more interesting corporate shows I've done.

Fairvue Plantation: Gallatin, TN

Fairvue Plantation is a private and astonishing community in Gallatin, TN, near Nashville. It features amazing houses, situated on a lake and golf course, with many other amenities to keep you happy year round.

I got booked there through one of my old friends, Stephen, who was their chef at the time. I was hired to do around 45 minutes, fairly clean, to the members of this private community.

When Jenny and I arrive, we are immediately overwhelmed by the beauty of this community. We pull into the clubhouse, and are greeted by Stephen. He gives us keys to our house for the night. Yes, you read that right. Jenny and I were treated to our own private house on the golf course. He also asked what we wanted for dinner. Filet, Bison, Lobster, whatever we wanted. Jenny looked at me and said "Book more of these shows, please."

We walk over to our house, which is a beautiful 2 story home situated on the 9th hole near the clubhouse. There is a porch overlooking the green. Wine waiting on us, along with some food and snacks. For a brief moment, I thought I was famous.

About an hour before the show, we go over to the clubhouse to enjoy an incredible dinner with Stephen. People are filing in, and I can overhear them saying "I hope he's dirty" and "I hope he's not one of those filthy comics." Oh, this is going to be interesting.

Finally, it's my time to do my thing. The place is packed. It's set up as a U shape, with a stairwell in the middle. There are stairs leading up to where we were from the bottom level, directly in front of me.

I had written my set to start off G rated, and eventually leading up to a slight R. That's what they asked for, so that's what I planned on.

During the clean part, they were laughing. Not hysterically, but they were laughing and were a fun group. It was time for me to ramp it up and bring out the harder stuff. Oh, timing, you are so funny.

Just as I'm doing my first "slightly dirty" bit, a woman and her kids walk up the stairs into the room. Luckily, I saw them, and stopped dead in my tracks. The room, however, didn't see them, and thought something was wrong with me. Once they realized that those kids may or may not have heard something they shouldn't have, they erupted. The rest of the show would be a blast.

After the show, while sitting at the bar, signing books for the members, the bartender hands us a bottle of good wine. He says "Enjoy. It's on us."

Jenny and I then walked back to our house on the 9th green. We had an amazing dinner, a great and eventful show, sold books, and now a bottle of great wine. We sat on the porch, with the moonlight, and had one of the deepest discussions we've ever had, while sitting in rocking chairs. I think I could do a show like that every night.

Sevier County High School Reunion Shows

I graduated from Sevier County High School in 1991. 20 years later, there I was, in front of my friends, telling jokes and funny stories, for money. Then, the next year, I was in front of the class of 1992, doing the same thing. Talk about a weird experience.

My own 20 year reunion was at the Edgewater Hotel in Gatlinburg. I must say....this was by far the most nervous I had ever been for a show. My 20 year High School reunion, 45 minutes, PG-13. I'd only been doing comedy a little over a year. Yet they all thought I was a professional comedian. What had I gotten myself into!

An hour before the show, I'm sitting in the lobby. I start seeing friends from so long ago. They are excited. I'm frightened. I was mad at myself for agreeing to this. What had I done?

Once the show starts, though, I'm fine. I do my thing. I have so much fun interacting with my friends from many years ago. I think they saw me as me, like I always was, but now with a microphone. It was High School all over again, but we had kids to go home to. To me, that was the only difference.

One year later, I got booked to perform at the 1992 Sevier County High School 20 year reunion. Although it was a class behind me, I had just as many friends there.

This one was at the Park Vista Hotel in Gatlinburg, situated up high on a hill, near some of the hiking trails for the Smoky Mountains. This night would get interesting before the show even started.

Trying to figure out which direction to take this show. 1992 Sevier County High School Reunion.

A half hour before it's my time to go up, Jenny and I go outside of the hotel to go over my set. This is my usual pre show scenario. I go outside, pace, breath, and clear my head. This one, however, would take a weird twist.

The double doors we went out of to go outside were roughly 75 yards from the doors to the conference room where the reunion was. Jenny and I walk down the corridor, out the doors, and they close behind us. There are a couple of cars there, surrounded by woods. Deep, heavy woods.

I pull out my set list, which was on a crumpled piece of paper. I start going over it. Jenny is standing near the doors. I'm pacing back and forth, as usual. Next thing we know, there is a bear, right there, next to us. Like, right there.

We kind of panicked? We were at the end of a long hallway, and we knew we had locked ourselves out. Nobody else was around. It's Jenny, myself, a couple of cars, a bear, and complete darkness.

After about 30 seconds of fear, Jenny grabs the door. Somehow, it wasn't locked. We survived. I rewrite my set to include almost just getting eaten by a bear.

Big smiles from Jenny and I, you know, after surviving almost getting eaten by a bear.

The show was fun. I did my set, in 2 parts. We danced and sang and hung out in between. It was different. I'm looking forward to hopefully being the entertainment for our next set of reunions. They are definitely worth it.

The Engineers and Funeral Home Employees

I know you might be confused reading that headline. These were back to back shows, in 2014. Engineers one night, Funeral Home employees the next. Apparently, I'll do anything.

The first show of this crazy weekend was at the Crowne Plaza, one of the nicer hotels in downtown Knoxville. 200+ engineers. Conference room. I would start performing while everyone got in line for the buffet dinner. Great.

I had been told, a million times, that engineers don't like to laugh. Everyone told me that, even the engineers themselves before the show started. I took that as a challenge.

Usually when I do corporate shows, I like to write 5 to 10 minutes of material specific to that company or at least the profession. I was very careful with the engineers as to not sound stupid. I think I ended up sounding stupid anyway, but it worked.

After I finished my set, I went out into the lobby to set up my book table. I was next to a small cash bar that was basically just a woman and a podium stand. It was a long hallway with a balcony overlooking the downstairs entrance. I waited and waited while they did their end of the year awards and other speeches and presentations. I think the woman working the bar felt sorry for me. She hooked me up.

Finally, the double doors open up from where they were having the party. I was out of books, but I was ready to take orders. Honestly, I wasn't sure if they would buy any. There were so many people, and I knew they would be rushing out the doors to get to the bar. Plus, I didn't know how funny I was. Yes, they were laughing, but not like a usual crowd. This was an engineer crowd laughing. It was different. It was hard to gauge.

The first few people walk out, come up to me, and said they had a good time. No book sales at first. Then, like a crazy rush, people started asking to order a copy. One after another. I was writing down names and addresses at a rapid pace. I was stunned. I guess they liked my set.

My book table after the show with the engineers. Waiting on the rush of people to exit the conference room.

It all started as a night of fear, performing for people who weren't supposed to laugh, yet it ended as a huge confidence boost. I thought "If I can make over 200 engineers laugh throughout my set, then who cares what tomorrow will bring?" Yeah, I was feeling pretty good. I should have known.

The next day, I wake up and start preparing for that night's show. A room full of funeral home employees from across the country. I mean, how hard could that be after all those engineers, right?

I get dressed up. I throw on a suit with a sweater vest. I get to the Ruth Criss Steakhouse in Knoxville, not exactly sure of what I had got myself into. I sit in the lobby. I'm next to a Christmas Tree made of wine bottles. The entire place is festive.

As I'm sitting on the little bench, an older crowd, in suits and evening gowns, arrives. They are surrounding me. I'm sitting there, with my little box for my book display, which I was still out of. I finally hear one of them mention a funeral home, so I know it's my people.

Finally, after 20 minutes, the hostess takes us downstairs to a large room. The wait staff already knows everyone. Apparently this was an annual thing here. I meet the people who hired me, and soon learn it will be a while before I go up. Everyone has to eat, formal announcements, etc. I notice there isn't a stage, or anything even closely resembling a stage. This is going to be interesting.

On top of that, it seems that I had a massive sinus infection going on. I was in the bathroom blowing my nose every 5 minutes. As I would walk out of the bathroom, a funeral home employee would go in. This would go on for almost 2 hours before it was my turn to perform.

I had been preparing for this show all day. I incorporated 15 minutes of new material, specifically funeral home related. I was hired to do 45 minutes. I was ready.

Finally, it's go time. They introduce me. As she hands me the microphone, she says to me "Oh, by the way....don't do any jokes about death or funeral homes." Well, there goes my first 15 minutes! I almost freaked out. However, I quickly composed myself, reconfigured my brain, and did 45 minutes of PG. No stage. Just standing in between tables while they ate. Probably not my best show ever, but I did my job. They laughed. It was a tough one, though.

Afterwards, 2 older gentlemen told me to come outside with them for a minute. We get outside, on this amazing balcony, overlooking the river. I'm trying to figure out what just happened. They said "Boy...what a tough room. You did great. Just figured you needed some air haha!" They were correct. It was an interesting show, to say the least. I was sent away with a check and tons of food. Another successful night.

Shows Without A Category

Sometimes, as a comedian trying to make it, you end up in places that just don't fall into a traditional category. Not a comedy club, bar, charity event, corporate show, or any other traditional venue. This is probably true for all types of entertainers as well. You gotta do what you gotta do.

Knoxville Comedy Cruise: Knoxville Riverboat

I was so excited. I was headlining the Knoxville Riverboat show, one of the longest standing shows in East Tennessee. This was going to be first experience making people laugh while moving on the water. Unfortunately, only half of my dream would come true.

Jenny and I arrived at the waterfront. The parking lot on the end where the boat was docked was pretty empty. It's about an hour before the boat is to take off and the show to begin. After a while, it becomes apparent that the crowd that evening would be on the light side. Come to find out, there is a sold out concert for George Strait right across the street at Thompson-Boling Arena. That's where everyone was. Well, at least that's what I've been telling myself all this time.

As the show gets closer to starting, we have around forty something people in the audience. Initially, I thought, that's not too bad. I've done shows for much, much smaller crowds. However, I find out that the boat won't move unless there are at least 50 people. Great.

So, Jenny and I hit the streets trying to find people. When I say streets, I mean the huge parking lot down to one of Knoxville's most popular restaurants, Calhoun's. We are trying to find people to come to the show. No luck. I'm about to do a show on a Riverboat that isn't going to move. At all. Figures.

The beautiful and historic Knoxville Riverboat. The same boat that I headlined that didn't move because not enough people showed up. Still a fun night.

The show went on. It was great. The boat didn't move, but it didn't matter. Everyone that showed up had fun. The comics, the audience, the staff (well, I'm not sure if they had fun or not to be honest.)

Yes, while I was on stage, I kept looking out the window to see if the boat was moving. It never did. I pretended it was, though. I think I may have even faked sea sickness. It was a night to remember, that's all I know.

Dick's Last Resort: Gatlinburg, TN

Oh, Dick's Last Resort, you. By far, one of the most interesting string of shows I've ever been a part of.

Dick's Last Resort is a restaurant chain where the wait staff is sarcastic and mean to its customers. It's a fun experience and unlike any other restaurant out there.

In 2014, I was asked by John, the manager at Dick's in Gatlinburg, if I would be interested in doing stand-up comedy shows there. Of course I was! Gatlinburg was, and still is, in dire need of stand-up comedy. For several months, twice a week, we gave it to them.

Dick's in Gatlinburg is a very large, 2 story restaurant, right next door to where I work my day job. The people who work there are wonderful and good friends of mine. We have spent many hours in the alley between our businesses talking about tourists. So, needless to say, it was an easy transition for me to go invade their turf and tell jokes. They welcomed me, and even joined in the fun.

Now, that's not to say there weren't a few hiccups along the way. They had never had stand-up comedy at that location before, and I had never had to set up my own PA system before either. There were nights where we were missing a microphone, a cord, etc. It worked out. I yelled out loud a couple times. My good friends from the band Autumn Reflection would help me out when they could. Tyler, Steve, and Justin would regularly bring me equipment at the last minute to get us going. By the way, Tyler, I still have your mic in my trunk.

For a majority of the shows, I would be the headliner. This was not the original design. However, after a few shows, the reputation was spreading. It was a tough gig. The crowd was loud, it was a PG show with many kids, the employees at Dick's were a part of the show, throwing chairs and sometimes louder than us, even though we had a microphone. It wasn't easy.

However, we were getting paid for an hour and a half show. I remember one night, after the emcee, a guest spot, and the feature were done, I looked at my watch. I still had an hour and 9 minutes to fill. PG. That's how tough it was.

Tyler Sonnichsen making the crowd laugh. When I say crowd, I mean that couple to his right. The other two people pictured is Debby Johnson, our emcee, and her daughter. Yeah. 2 people. We did the entire hour and a half, too, and they left happy.

One of the aspects of Dick's that separates it from any other show I've done is the fact that 100% of the crowd consisted of tourists. From New York, L.A., Alabama, Hawaii, Saudi Arabia, Japan. All tourists. Different crowd every night. Sometimes tons of kids. Sometimes zero kids. Sometimes hecklers and drunk groups. Sometimes all nice families who were shy. You really never knew what you were getting until the show started. Could be 2 people. Or it could be 120. It was very random. Many of the comics hated it. The more I did it, the more I looked forward to the challenge.

After performing for my boys, niece, and nephew. From left to right: Hudson, Ethan, Brayden, Briana, and Jacob. They enjoyed it so much, they asked to come back many times. I asked that they didn't. Horrible hecklers.

Many of the comics from the Knoxville scene and around Tennessee performed at Dick's in those few months. Hunter Roberts, Grady Ray, Matt Ward, Tyler Sonnichsen, Nate Cate, Mike Howard, Debby Johnson, Gail Grantham Moore, Boston McCown, Lance Adams, Christopher Seaton, John Upton, J.D. Howard, Jake James Hasenauer, Shane Rhyne, Chase Dyer, and myself braved this show week in and week out. I can't speak for the rest of them, but I know that I gained more stage skills during that time span than I have the last 5 years combined. Maybe I can put together a reunion show sometime soon. I'll probably be the only one there though. Well, except Debby and Gail. They always came. They literally saved me 10 times when I was short a comic. Oh, Sevier County and its' comedy.

Metro Wines: Asheville, NC

Oh, let's see. How do we put Alex in a tough situation to perform? I know, let's put him in an amazing wine store, knowing that he can't drink wine, which is one of his passions, and speak clearly into a microphone. Torture.

I'll admit. I had no idea what I was getting myself into when I booked this show. All I knew is that Jenny wanted to go to Asheville and that the word "wine" was in the venue's title. So, yeah, no brainer.

When we arrived to a packed parking lot, I was extremely excited! As usual, we were an hour early and I couldn't believe there were that many people there already. I thought to myself "Man...I must have written a great bio for their website!"

As we get closer to the door of Metro Wines, we start seeing people exit, with dogs. I looked at Jenny, who, being an animal lover, was now beaming with curiosity, and I said "What..in...the...?"

I peek inside and there are more people with dogs! Beautiful Greyhounds to be exact. At this point, Jenny had completely forgotten that I was performing and immediately ditched me to go pet the dogs. I realized this was going to be an interesting night. I also realized, while standing dumfounded on the sidewalk, that all the cars in the parking lot were actually there for the bar next door. There were almost more dogs in the wine store than people. So, I immediately started writing new jokes that only dogs would laugh at.

As we get inside and start looking around, meeting the owners and having a glass or two of wine (I know....I shouldn't try this again...but, oh well), I'm starting to catch a groovy vibe about this place. At the same time, I'm trying to figure out where the actual stage is going to be. There was a wall of wine separating the tables and chairs that were set up. Yep...this was going to be a different kind of show.

I had a book table set up right next to the front doors. I was sitting there, with Jenny, signing books before the show while sipping wine in a wine store. I wanted this to be my new profession. Forget the comedy part. Just sip wine and sign books in wine stores.

There were 2 guys opening for me that I didn't know. The host was a good friend of mine, Tom Scheve from Asheville, who I've had the pleasure of working with on numerous occasions around the southeast. The crowd started filing in slowly, but steadily. All the dogs eventually left. So much for those canine funnies I had written in the parking lot. As the show begins, the first comic tells an offensive joke about dogs, riling up the crowd. Yeah comedy!

Surrounded by wine at Metro Wines in Asheville, NC. What an awesome store. Go there if you get the chance!

By the time I go up to headline the show, the place was full. All the seats, on both sides of the wall of wine, the tasting bar, and a few standing. Being that this was my first show inside a wine store, and that I consider myself an amateur wine connoisseur, I had prepared a good 10 to 15 minutes of material that was relatable. I had practiced some very intense and difficult wine names, and I actually pulled them off without a slip. I think I was more excited about that than all of the laughs. Ok, I wasn't really, but maybe.

After the show, I sold several more books, met a lot of interesting people, and was helped by the owners in picking out some special wines for us to buy and take home. It was a great night.

I'm not sure if they still do shows there anymore, but if they do, I can't wait to go back. What started as a "what have I got myself into?" moment turned into a "I could do this every night" kind of show.

First Night Knoxville: Knoxville, TN

Have you ever found yourself so unprepared for something that you were absolutely terrified? Welcome to my experience as being the featured entertainment for Knoxville's big New Year's Eve show downtown. Oh, and I should mention, I had only been doing stand-up comedy for a little over a year at this point.

When I was first asked by Knoxville's own media celebrities Erin Donavan and Frank Murphy to perform, I was overcome with excitement. I immediately pictured a bunch of drunk people celebrating New Year's downtown, partying and enjoying my edgier comedy style that I possessed at that time. Nope. I was wrong.

The day before the show, or December 30th as most people seem to call it, I sent Erin a message to get the details. What is the exact location, how many people, length of my set, etc. I was an inexperienced comic at the time, and waited until the last minute to ask for this important information. Big mistake...that I would never make again. Ok...that's a lie. I think you've read about a few of them already. Oh, and there might be another one or 2 coming.

I am told by Erin that it's a HUGE auditorium downtown at the TVA building. I need to do 25 minutes or so, for 2 shows, with over 400 people at each one. Oh, and it must be G rated since there would be many kids in attendance. What???!!!! Oh no...on so many levels.

First of all, at that point in my so called career, I had never performed in front of more than 200 people. Second, I had never done a show with kids in attendance. Maybe PG-13 here or there, but definitely not G. Last, I had 24 hours to write a brand new 25 minute G rated set from scratch. Time to test my skills Mr. (I think those were the exact words I said to myself in the bathroom mirror after I read the message from Erin.)

As I arrive, shaking, I see a packed house. The stage is huge, way bigger than anything I had been on before. There were flags lining the entire length of the stage. State flags, United Stats Flags, etc. What was this place? Where was I? Who are all these people and why are they here? Why are there ushers? Help me somebody! I want to quit doing comedy right now forever! Please help me not do comedy anymore especially tonight! Where is the bathroom! Help!

I finally run into Frank backstage. I'm sure he could tell I was out of my element and slightly nervous. He assured me everything would be ok.

After he introduces me, I stumble through the curtain onto the monstrous stage. I trip, repeatedly, over the microphone cord, the speakers, and anything else that got in front of me, behind me, or within 100 yards. I stare out into the crowd. Now, let me tell you, at this particular point in my career I had not mastered the art of the "blank stare." This is where you pick 3 points in the audience, go back and forth between them, without ever looking at anyone in particular. No, on this night, I could see EVERYBODY, especially the 30 kids ages 4 through 13 in the front row! I wasn't liking it, I'll tell you that much. Here goes nothing.

I muff the first joke, bad. However, I quickly gained my composure and made them laugh the rest of the time, even the kids. I was very proud of myself. I had pulled this whole thing off in 24 hours. It was the first time I actually thought that I could make money doing the whole comedy thing.

After the shows were over, and a couple weeks went by, I really started to focus on writing some PG material. I had this odd feeling, or premonition. that somewhere down the road it would pay off. I was already optimistic that I would be successful someday at comedy, but for some reason, after this night, I thought that the whole "clean show" thing would be a money maker. I never imagined that a few years later that would come true, especially in front of crowds like funeral home employees and engineers in ritzy ballrooms and country clubs. Life is so weird.

This is a close up shot of me performing at First Night Knoxville's New Year's Eve show. You wouldn't believe how big this room was and how big the crowd was. Oh, and that stage!

Elk's Lodge: Knoxville, TN

Here is another example of a show that ended up being great, although my expectations going in were low to say the least. This show had it all: A strong line up of comics, an intriguing and "secretive" feeling location, and a packed room. I felt like I was in a movie or something, performing for the rich in some hidden club.

The people there were great. I already knew some of them, so the pre-show mingling was fun as always. The comedians for that night included myself, Sandy Goddard, Danny Whitson, Karen George, Tyler Gooch, and Marcus Griffin. Definitely a wide variety of styles in that group.

The room itself was huge, with a tiny little stage on one side. Yes, I did fall off, twice. People were mostly sitting at tables, packed all around the stage and pretty far back. I wasn't really sure what to expect, or what type of material was going to work with this crowd. I had been told to keep the language in check. Luckily, I was going on near the end, so I was able to scope out the audience's reactions to the other comics. I always watch the crowd's faces after Marcus. That's usually a good gauge on what not to say.

Trying my best not to fall off the little stage at the Elks Lodge in Knoxville. I wasn't completely successful.

It didn't take long to figure out that they wanted it a little more risqué than I was originally told. So, we spiced it up a bit. Sold quite a few books after the show, made some new contacts that led to some corporate shows down the road, and had a blast hanging out in the secret club with my friends. Another successful night.

Sandy Goddard, myself, Danny Whitson, Marcus Griffin, Karen George, and Tyler Gooch. Fun night at the Elks Lodge.

The Top 3 Weirdest Shows

Sometimes, you just never know what you are getting into until you find yourself standing there with that feeling of being naked in front of the class. Well, I've had that happen a handful of times over the last 5 years. Here are my top 3 weirdest shows.

The Women's Expo: Sevierville, TN

So, yeah, I agreed to do a free show for a womens' expo in Sevierville. It was during the day, in a big room that had a stage to one side. The building was used for many functions, such as Chamber of Commerce meetings and things of that nature. There were tables set up all around the room where the women were selling household items, food, kitchen supplies, jewelry, etc. They were also doing cooking demonstrations to the right of the stage. There were several kids there as well. It was about as awkward a situation as I've ever found myself in. And Jenny was laughing at me the entire time.

For roughly an hour, before it was time for me to perform, I was trying to figure out exactly what I was supposed to be doing. Traditional stand up? Motivational speaking? PG was obvious. I at least figured that part out with the kids running around and everything.

They had several rows of chairs set up in front of the stage. They had been having other speakers periodically, with a wide variety of topics, mostly geared towards women. Every minute that went by, I was eliminating another joke or bit from what I had originally planned. By the time they called for me to go up, I was completely clueless as to what I was going to say. Literally nothing. For the first time ever, I was blank. Zero funny stuff going on in my brain. Jenny was still laughing.

Finally, after a brief introduction, I grab the mic. I'm supposed to do around 20 to 30 minutes. Of what? Yeah, still not sure at that point. I'm thinking it might be best to do some immediate crowd work. My crowd, however, consisted of several kids in front of the stage, 2 or 3 people in the chairs, and the rest were still sitting at their booths and tables selling merchandise.

The mic works for about 8 seconds before it goes out. The batteries died. Whew! I got a break. This will give me a little time to check out the room and find something, anything, to say.

Now, Jenny is losing her composure in the corner. I really think she enjoyed watching me squirm up there. Here I am, in a weird room, with a very random crowd, in the middle of the afternoon, holding a broken microphone with nothing at all to say.

Finally, after about 6 tries, the mic works. I decided to just tell my story of growing up and becoming a comedian, as well as a little local humor from my book. Everything was going well, or at least as well as it could have. Until...I slipped up and did a joke that was not exactly G rated. It wasn't bad, but it wasn't exactly 100% kid friendly. Well, talking about awkward silence. I bit my lip. I turned around, facing the back of the stage. Next thing I hear is a blender in the side kitchen as they were doing a cooking demonstration. Wow, I just got saved by cake mix!

I stumbled through the rest of it, got some strange laughter (probably just Jenny), and walked off the stage relieved. Grabbed a brownie from Kim, who booked me for the expo, and we got in the car. I looked at her, she looked at me, and we busted out laughing. Then I burned the tires out of the parking lot.

Boots N Spurs: Bristol, TN

I'm already having a hard time typing this without laughing.

I don't think a show like this can ever be duplicated. It had it all.

I was booked to headline this show, again, by my good friend J. C. Ratliff. Bristol is about an hour and a half drive from Knoxville. This was a new show that was starting up, and I would have the honor of getting to do my thing there.

Performing with me that night were my good friends Jake James Hasenour, J. D. Howard, and J.C. Pretty strong show right there.

As Jenny and I arrive in Bristol, a huge storm is brewing up in the sky. It's turning black. We wind through all of these backroads, following the GPS and looking for a shopping center. Finally, we arrive to this huge, mostly empty parking lot. We see a few businesses that seem like they are open. One appears to be a bowling alley. The other, with a multi-colored strobe light in the doorway, appears to be Boots N Spurs. Here we go.

Early as usual, we go in through the strobe light filled hallway. Jenny is giving me that "what have you booked yourself into this time?" look. I'm giving her that "let's just wait and see what happens?" look. We do this often. Her look is usually more accurate than mine, however.

J.C, J.D, and Jake are there. Along with 4 people sitting at the bar. There is one bartender, and she appears to also be the owner.

Now, I'm not sure what this place used to be, but it's big and weird. The décor is obviously boots n spurs themed, whatever that is. Horns on the wall, etc. It's a very large room, although only a tiny part was being utilized by the 4 people. The stage was initially going to be the dance floor, surrounded by mirrors, in the corner. However, it became apparent that the 4 people at the bar had no intention of moving.

We wait for more people to show up. I think we capped it off at 7 people? All of them at the bar. So, in a last second decision, the stage will now be on top of the bar. This night just keeps getting weirder and weirder.

J.C., Jake, and J.D. get on the bar, one at a time, and do their thing. I was in such shock, I failed to even notice if anyone was laughing. I'm sure they were, but I was zoned out.

Finally, I get up. I was originally supposed to do 45 minutes to an hour, but I'm already thinking about cutting this one down to about 30. The weather was bad, there were 7 uninterested people there, and I was standing on top of a bar in a place called Boots N Spurs. Yeah, let's cut it a little short.

Somehow, during the entire night and watching the other 3 guys perform, I had failed to notice that there was a go kart sized race car dangling from the ceiling, right above the bar, which is now the stage. As I'm getting started with my set, I immediately have to duck and dodge this thing. My entire comedy career flashed before my eyes. Not because I almost got a concussion, but because I realized that I was standing on a bar telling jokes to 7 people and almost hit my head on a car. Yeah, um, career.

As you can see, my head wasn't as close to the car as it felt when I was up there. Either way, there are really no other words for this scenario.

As if it couldn't get any weirder, in the middle of my set, Jake James had convinced some guy to eat the pickled eggs that were in a huge jar sitting on the bar. So, I just stopped for an intermission to watch this guy shove these things in his mouth. I think everyone there, including myself, was more entertained by this spectacle than our show. After the guy lets me know he's done, I finish my set.

The coolest thing was, J.C. still paid me. With what money? I have no idea. Probably his own. That's why I'll always do shows for him when asked. Also, because when he and I do something together it usually ends up weird. Oh, Boots N Spurs, I'll never forget you.

The Jefferson City Events Center: Jefferson City, TN

If you thought that Boots N Spurs show sounded weird, then wait until you hear this story. Wow. Just wow. And, it was all my fault.

In 2014, I was contacted on Facebook by my friends Kyle Adkins and Sherry Bryant about doing a charity benefit show for the Jefferson City Events Center. Jefferson City is only about a half hour or so from Knoxville. I of course agreed, and put together a strong line-up of comics, consisting of Mike Howard, Boston McCown, and Shane Rhyne. It was going to be an exciting show, I was sure of it.

Mike is not only a comic, but also an actor and well known radio host in Knoxville. So, I wanted to have a celebrity host the event, and he was the perfect choice. Boston and Shane are both great comedians, with very different styles. So, together, the 4 of us were going to put on one incredible show at the Jefferson City Events Center.

Let's start making this weird now, what do you say? So, Jenny and I put the address for the Events Center in our GPS. We finally get to the street, but all we see are old, rundown buildings. When I say run down, I mean there were collapsed buildings, water damage, fire damage, graffiti, etc. It looked like a warzone. It was also right next to train tracks, so it felt like it was a part of an abandoned business district in a big city. However, the GPS said we were at the right place.

So, Jenny and I are creeping along in our car, looking for any sign of life. I park on the side of the street. Up ahead, we see an opening in between two buildings. It looks like there was a building there at one time, but now just an empty lot, kind of like a wide alley. As we looked closer, we see a trailer bed parked in the front close to the street. Also, we see Kyle and Sherry sitting in chairs with a party tent. What is going on?

Jenny gives me that "look" again. I'm confused. So, I walk up to Kyle and Sherry while Jenny sits in the car. I find out the Events Center hasn't actually been built yet, and that this was an outdoor fundraiser to raise money to build and renovate! So, I have to walk back to tell Jenny that I messed up.

Here's what happened. When they first asked me to do the show, I agreed. I looked at the Facebook page for the Events Center, and it they had over 17,000 likes. Also, it had a seating capacity of over 1,500. I didn't read that it WAS NOT built or renovated yet. I got so excited about performing in a venue that big that I totally disregarded the rest of the description. I then booked Boston, Shane, and Mike to come to this huge fundraising event in an arena that sat 1,500. It was a HUGE deal.

So, now that you know that it was my fault because I didn't read everything I should have and ended up preparing for a show that wasn't actually like it seemed, let me tell you the rest of the story.

I also learned from Kyle and Sherry that they were having a hard time finding people to attend the event. At that point, literally, they were the entire audience. So, I told them that I would go out and try to find people and that I would be back in a while.

I got in the car, explained the situation to Jenny, she laughed, hysterically, and we drove off. I immediately called Mike and told him "there is not a show. Do not come! It might only be like 2 people. I'll just do it!" He said "Oh no, I'm on the way, and we are doing this, and we are going to have fun!"

I had no luck getting a hold of Boston or Shane. They were all coming, and it was going to be interesting.

The crowd is starting to file in for the big alley show.

We do everything we can to get people there. Stopping cars, Facebook, Twitter, anything. We end up with a total of 7 people. That included a couple kids and a dog. So I should have said 7 living things came to our show.

In the actual lot we were in, we had chairs set up near the stage. Nobody sat there. Instead, they all sat upon a high wall near the back, nowhere even close to us. There was one lady who came and went and kind of wandered around in the alley with her grand kids. That was about it though.

Shane Rhyne posing on the flatbed trailer before the show starts. Eventually, 6 people and a dog would show up and sit on the wall behind where Shane is in this picture.

I told the guys "Hey...just do whatever and let's get out of here. Don't worry about doing your scheduled time limits. Seriously, just do whatever." I felt bad.

They all responded that "we are doing this show. We are taping it. This is going to be one to remember." And, we did. Mike warmed up the crowd, including the dog. Shane and Boston did their entire sets. Then, Jenny tells me "Just hurry. Don't do very much."

I ended up doing at least 45 minutes. I have no clue what I was saying. A train went by. An airplane almost hit us I think. The dog left. The wandering grandmother and her kids, whose car was just parked in the middle of the street, left. We all had fun. We let loose, made the best of an awkward situation, and ended up having one of the most interesting experiences I've had so far as a comedian. It was just one of those nights.

After I got done, I decided that since we already had a tent and a table, that I would set up a merch table for my books. Yeah, I knew it was a joke and that nobody would buy one, but I did it anyway. Before I left the stage, I had told the 5 people who were left that I had books for sale. Why? I don't know.

So, we are all standing around talking afterwards. We are laughing about the entire situation. About 10 minutes later, right before I pack up my books, the people who were sitting on the wall for the show came up out of nowhere. They wanted to buy a couple books. They literally had to walk 2 blocks to get to us. It was either that or jump off the wall to the main stage.

Unfortunately, their only form of payment could only be accepted at a certain department store. Just my luck. At least I felt like I gave them a good show since they wanted to buy them.

We thanked Kyle and Sherry for having us and told them if they ever needed us again, don't hesitate to call. We had so much fun. You never know how something is going to go until you just do it. Lesson learned.

This did not help sell any books, just in case you were wondering.

On The Road With Jenny

This chapter is the epitome of what this book is about. Husband. Father. Comedian. Yeah.

So, in 2014 Jenny and decided to do a short tour. Really, we just wanted a long vacation. I would tell jokes along the way to unfamiliar crowds in several states. We would hit the beaches, shop, and just lounge around the rest of the time. 2 weeks in Alabama, Georgia, Florida, and Louisiana. It was going to be awesome. We already had 7 shows lined up.

Well, as usual, kid schedules, work schedules, and the lack of money intervened. What started as a 2 week vacation in 8 cities with 7 shows, ended as a 5 day vacation with 2 shows in 2 cities.

Disappointed, we thought "We'll take it! Now please!"

You see, we don't get much time to ourselves. We have 4 boys with 3 separate exes. We both work regular jobs. Jenny is going back to school. I do comedy at night. I also coach or attend all my kid's basketball games. It's a hectic life. So, yeah, 5 days to ourselves! Perfect!

The first stop would be Tallahassee, FL, for a show at Bird's Aphrodisiac and Oyster Shack. Yeah, I'm sure you are as intrigued by the name as I was.

We were both excited about the trip. Outside of Tennessee, except maybe a couple different times, I had not traveled as a "headliner." This would be a show in a state where nobody knows me. I wasn't nervous, but more intrigued. I was interested to see how many people would come out, how they would react to my style, and how I would be received in general.

I had already heard good things about the 2 actual shows that I was going to get to do on this shortened "tourcation." The first one, I would be headlining an open mic in a bar. The second was a more traditional show, also in a bar. So, this trip would be a good mix of different shows.

After we check into our hotel in Tallahassee, Jenny and I decide to get ready and do some sight-seeing before the show. We were both craving good burgers and ended up at Vertigo Burgers and Fries. Very good, I must say.

We then drive closer to where Bird's is located. It just happens to be on or around the Florida State University campus, which is beautiful. We drive by the venue, just to check it out. There are a lot of people there. It seems to be a small place, but looks like fun nevertheless.

We keep driving for a bit, taking in the wonderful scenery of the campus. Jenny makes me stop and take some pictures, which she knows that I hate doing. Finally, we head back for the show. As we pull up, we can hardly get a parking spot. Wow. Was not expecting that!

We finally go in and grab some seats at the bar. The place is already crowded. Scott Peavy, who runs this show and booked me, does a great job of packing the place on Wednesday nights. It was a much younger crowd than what I was used to, so I was kind of excited about trying some different stuff I hadn't planned on.

As the show begins, the place is absolutely packed. People standing around the perimeter of the entire bar. Jenny and I were lucky to even get a seat. We set up the books at our table, near the door, and caught stares of "who is this guy?" all night long as people walked by. It's a weird feeling, before you go up on stage, to have your book out for sale and nobody has a clue who you are or why you have these books sitting on the table.

There were quite a few comics there that night, and I honestly can't remember how long each one did. Maybe 5 to 7 minutes. The crowd itself was definitely there to see comedy. For a bar setting, it was relatively quiet and people were laughing. I was really getting excited about this one as it went along.

Before I hit the stage, I saw this. It's really tough to use the restroom while staring at yourself.

Now, Jenny is always honest with me after I do a set. She has been one of the biggest assets to the advancement of my career as a stand-up comedian. She critiques me, tells me when something doesn't work, or if it needs to be changed, etc. She's even written a few punchlines here or there that took a particular bit to a new level. I'm not going to tell you which ones so I don't have to give her specific credit.

So, on this particular night at Bird's Aphrodisiac Shack in Tallahassee, I got yelled at pretty hard. She was not happy with me. Apparently (she didn't have to yell at me, I already knew), I decided to feed off the other comics before me, which I had never done before. They had all been pretty dirty or "blue" as comics call it. Not that I am clean by any means, but I kind of went over the top thinking that's what the audience wanted. I got laughs, but it wasn't my normal kind of laughs. I wasn't doing my bits and jokes like I usually do. I was cranking them up to a point that they weren't funny anymore.

All in all though, it was a fun show. I would love to go back there again and be myself. Scott does a great job and the venue is very comedy friendly with great food and drinks!

Fun night at Bird's Aphrodisiac Shack in Tallahassee, FL.

The next morning, Jenny and I packed our bags to make the 3 hour drive to Pensacola, FL, for my next show at the Big Easy Tavern. For a couple years, I had been hearing great things about this show, and I was excited to get to finally headline it. Until then, though, Jenny and I would get a day to ourselves.

This was the first time I had been to the Pensacola area in 20 years. I was born in the area, and always loved it, so it was a neat feeling to be going back there to perform. Jenny and I spent that Thursday at Navarre Beach and then Pensacola Beach, before hitting our hotel inland. As usual, we missed the kids and wished they were there to be at the beach with us. Well, for the most part. Not so much when we sitting on the beach eating fish tacos at 4pm without any stress. We very rarely are stressless it seems.

That night we were free, so we went out on the town. We ended up at Seville Quarter, a huge and amazing night club that had a little bit of everything. It was a multi room venue, and we kind of just lost ourselves. We were 21 again having a blast. Especially loved those dueling pianos.

The next night was my show at the Big Easy Tavern created by the one and only Bubbs Harris. This show had a great reputation amongst traveling comics, at least from the ones I know who had done it from Knoxville. I had heard rumors that some nights it was a swinger bar, other nights a biker bar, other night's comedy. I had no idea what to expect, and zero clue if any of that was true.

After a relaxing day, Jenny and I arrive at the Big Easy Tavern, which is located at the bottom of a hotel. When we walk up, there are comics sitting outside, hanging out. Gar Harris, the host, greets us and takes us inside. As repetitive as this may sound, we are very early. When Jenny is with me, it's usually to get there to try their food. So, we did, and it was great.

The bar itself was fairly dark. It was not at all what I was expecting. The set up was very unique. The stage was straight across from the bar, with a sunken area in between for seats of all kinds. Booths, circular tables, etc. There was a pool table on one side, a row of chairs on the other along the wall. It was different, but comfortable.

The one and only Big Easy Tavern in Pensacola, FL. At the time, this show was run by Bubbs Harris, and was one of the best atmospheres for a bar show I had ever been a part of.

The crowd that night was good. It wasn't overly packed, but there were enough there for it to seem full. That's just the way the room was laid out. After my show a couple night's earlier, where I was not myself, I had decided to come out strong. Apparently it worked, because I was signing books for quite a while afterwards on the pool table. Jenny said that it may have been my best performance to date.

I'm not sure if they do shows there still. I'm just glad I got my chance to perform there that night, and if it was like that again, I'd go back. Plus, Jenny and I hit the Seville Quarter again afterwards, so there's that too. That was our last vacation. Hopefully Jenny and I will get another chance soon. This real life stuff is hard.

The Knoxville Comedy Scene

I thought it would be important to dedicate a chapter to the amazing comedy scene that we have here in Knoxville. When most people think of stand-up comedy, they think New York, L.A., or Chicago. Even regionally, people will mention Atlanta, Nashville, or Charlotte. All incredible cities crawling with great comedians, interesting venues, and many, many shows on a nightly basis. However, Knoxville, is quickly becoming more than a hidden gem in the comedy world.

When I first started in 2010, Side Splitters was really the only thing going on comedy wise in the Knoxville area. Not only was it the only true "comedy club", but it was the only consistent place to see a show, other than some of the biggest national headliners at either The Tennessee Theater or the Bijou Theater.

Side Splitters had a very strong base of comics at the time, many of which today are headlining, featuring, or running their own shows somewhere. The only competition amongst comics back then was for spots at the club, either as an emcee on the weekends, or getting a sporadic guest spot. Same people, for the most part, every single week at the open mics.

Not too long after I had started, Matt Ward, a fellow comedian, friend, and producer of shows and festivals in different parts of the country, began to expand the Knoxville comedy scene to other venues. Preservation Pub, which is still a weekly show every Sunday, to this day, was the beginning of what would become a plethora of shows almost every night of the week.

Early on, however, there would be some riffs between some comics and the management from Side Splitters and those who branched out to do the "underground" scene. Nothing major, and, from what I've heard, it's like that in every city. It's just the nature of the business. There are those who believe that comedy clubs are the only way to make it as a comedian. Then, there are those who don't like the structure and system of a comedy club. I was always one of the few "in between" guys. Being the nice guy that gets along with everyone, I often found myself having late night discussions online with fellow comics, calming nerves and putting out fires. Not as big of a deal as many thought, so I'm not going to spend any more time on it. Basically, comedians love drama for some reason. Let's just say that in the end, it has all worked out. Comedy in Knoxville is thriving.

It wasn't only "Knoxville" that was experimenting with shows at this time. We were branching out into other surrounding areas like Maryville, Oak Ridge, Gatlinburg, and Sevierville. Trying to make people laugh in bars, warehouses, restaurants, whatever. Some of those shows are still active today.

Here is a quick tribute to some of the shows of the past. I'm sure I missed some. It's best to play some soft music while reading this list.

Prince's Deli, Knoxville
The Bullpen, Alcoa
Patrick Sullivan's, Knoxville
The Buffalo Grille, Oak Ridge
Twisted Mike's, Knoxville
Just One More, Knoxville
The Relix Theater, Knoxville
Dick's Last Resort, Gatlinburg
Rocky Top Theater, Sevierville
The Well, Knoxville
Junction 33, Knoxville
The Station, Knoxville
The Thirsty Turtle, Maryville

Now, some of these shows were short lived. Some lasted over a year or more. They were mixes of open mics, showcases, contests, and regular shows. Ahhh....good times at all.

Matt would also start the Rocky Top Comedy Contest in Knoxville. Its first year was at the Relix Theater, and it has grown since. J.C. Ratliff also started the Old City Comedy Competition at Carleo's in the Old City. So, we now have 2 separate regional comedy contests to choose from. I have had the honor of competing in both of them, and I must say they are both extremely well organized and fairly judged.

The 2013 finals of the Rocky Top Comedy Contest at The Well. Myself onstage with the one and only Jeff Blank, one of Knoxville's top comedians.

In December of 2014, Side Splitters Comedy Club closed it's doors for good. It was up and down for a while, but had slowly been losing steam. By the time this happened, the rest of the Knoxville comedy scene was booming so much that the availability to find stage time for comics wasn't an issue. The opportunity to share the stage and learn from nationally touring headliners was the main loss with Side Splitters closing. Eventually, the riffs between the club comics and the underground comics would slowly fade away.

Also, in 2014, Matt started the Scruffy City Comedy Festival in downtown Knoxville. You've already read about it earlier, so I won't go into much detail again. However, the addition of this festival has opened up the eyes of comics from all over the country, and is just another step cementing Knoxville as a major player in the comedy world.

So, we have 2 great contests and a national comedy festival. What about the other shows you ask? Well, we have plenty, and they are all good.

(Note: This is a current list as of publication. Some of these may have changed, or there may be some new ones out there. If you are reading this in 2020, then I'm sorry, I can't help you.)

Open Mics

** Sundays
   Upstairs Underground Show at Preservation Pub, Knoxville
   Boston McCown

** Tuesdays
   Stand Up Saloon at Long Branch Saloon, Knoxville
   John Miller

** Fridays
   Knox Vegas Open Mic Comedy at Sassy Ann's, Knoxville
   Jay Kendrick

Showcase and Traditional Shows

** Tuesdays
  Old City Comedy at Carleo's in the Old City, Knoxville
  J.C. Ratliff

** 1st Tuesday Every Month
  Casual Comedy at The Casual Pint, Knoxville
  Shane Rhyne, Tyler Sonnichsen, Sean Simoneau,
  Matt Chadourne

** 1st Friday Every Month
  First Friday Comedy at Saw Works Brewing Company, Knoxville
  Shane Rhyne, Tyler Sonnichsen, Sean Simoneau,
  Matt Chadourne

** Spike Collar Comedy at Open Chord, Knoxville
  J.C. Ratliff

** Comedy at The Grove, Grove Theater, Oak Ridge
  Danny Whitson

** 1341 Comedy at Club 1341 Grill, Sevierville
  Alex Stokes

** Knoxville Comedy Cruise, Knoxville Riverboat
  Matt Ward

Specialty Shows

** Mondays
  QED Comedy Laboratory at The Pilot Light, Knoxville
  Matt Chadourne

** Tuesdays
  Einstein Simplified Improv at Scruffy City Hall, Knoxville

As you can see, Knoxville is thriving when it comes to making people laugh. There are other shows as well, sometimes at Scruff City Hall, Preservation Pub, and other venues that feature out of town headliners. All in all, there are plenty of opportunities for both fans and comics to see a show or perform.

The future is bright for comedy in East Tennessee. The venues, the variety of shows, and the comics themselves are one of a kind. Other projects, such as Victor Agreda Jr.'s short films with comics and his Scruffy Science CinePub 6000 show at Scruffy City Hall, as well as Sam Donnelly's documentary filming about comedy, only expand the menu of creative opportunities for us all. For myself, it's nice to have so many chances to perform close to home and not leave the family all the time.

So, whether or not you live in the area or are just passing through, catch a show. Or two. You won't be disappointed. For updated info, just visit www.scruffycitycomedy.com.

Scruffy City Hall, one of the many amazing venues where you can catch live Stand Up Comedy and Improv in Knoxville, TN.

What's Next?

Yeah, the million-dollar question. Where do I go next? Well, that's the fun part. Who knows?

6 years ago, I gave my last presentation in a small conference room to prospective clients about specific financial products. Since that day, I have been telling jokes to people in comedy clubs, bars, alleys, theaters, restaurants, and just about anywhere else you could imagine. I never, ever saw that coming.

So, how in the world can I predict where I'm going? Obviously, I keep working at what I'm doing now. That's a given. But, where is that going to take me? That's the exciting part. Just like walking into a bar, in another city, to tell jokes to a rowdy crowd. Unpredictability. I love it.

I've been fortunate to have a book already that has had so many people enjoy it. I have a wonderful family that supports me 100 percent. I have hundreds, if not thousands of friends in the comedy world, all over the country. I have so many friends who support me, come to shows, and promote me. I'm lucky to be close to my father, David, and my stepmother, Beverly, so they can see me perform often. Hopefully I can make it to Dallas soon so my mom and brother can see the real me, too.

I've worked hard to have whatever success I've had so far. I'm going to keep working hard, in all areas. That I know. I'm going to keep doing it *my* way. That I know. Where that takes me? That I don't know.

Comedy Clubs. Bars. Corporate Shows. Let's just do them all and see what happens.

My next book could be about doing shows in barns. Only barns. Stay tuned.